DATE DUE

GLOBAL ORGANIZATIONS

The World Bank and the International Monetary Fund

GLOBAL ORGANIZATIONS

GLOBAL ORGANIZATIONS

The World Bank and the International Monetary Fund

Meredith Lordan

Series Editor
Peggy Kahn
University of Michigan–Flint

CHELSEA HOUSE
PUBLISHERS
An imprint of Infobase Publishing

The World Bank and the International Monetary Fund

Chelsea House
An imprint of Infobase Publishing
132 West 31st Street
New York NY 10001

Library of Congress Cataloging-in-Publication Data
Lordan, Meredith.
The World Bank and the International Monetary Fund / Meredith Lordan.
    p. cm. — (Global organizations)
Includes bibliographical references and index.
ISBN 978-0-7910-9539-3 (hardcover)
ISBN 978-1-4381-1666-2 (e-book)
 1. World Bank. 2. International Monetary Fund. 3. Economic assistance. I. Title. II. Series.

HG3881.5.W57L67 2008
332.1'532—dc22   2008024016

Series design by Erik Lindstrom
Composition by Keith Trego
Cover design by Ben Peterson
Cover printed by Yurchak Printing, Landisville, Pa.
Book printed and bound by Yurchak Printing, Landisville, Pa.
Printed in the United States of America

CONTENTS

INTRODUCTION

Deepti in India

FIFTEEN-YEAR-OLD DEEPTI LIVES IN CHENNAI, FORMERLY called Madras, the capital city of the Indian state of Tamil Nadu. India's fourth largest city, Chennai was founded by the British colonial powers in the seventeenth century. Even before the start of British colonial rule, Chennai was led by various Indian dynasties as early as the first century. Although it continues to serve as an important administrative center today, glimpses of the not-too-distant colonial past may be seen in the Chennai city center. Reminiscent of a gingerbread house, the Central Train Station, with its rich cranberry-red hue with white edging, is an example of British-influenced architecture. The Central Train Station contrasts with the surrounding Hindu temples and blocks of concrete-and-glass modern office buildings. The colonial mixes with the local as a linguistic mixture of Tamil, Hindi, and English may be over-heard. Delicious aromas waft across the city center as vendors prepare food—including *masala dosai* (a thin, spiced pancake), *sambar* (pea and vegetable stew), *chutney* (a sweet and spicy condiment), and *daal* (lentil stew)—for pedestrians walking to and from Ranganathan Street, a famous shopping boulevard. With neon signs, dazzling light displays at night, and goods from around the world, Ranganathan Street is a vibrant place.

Not too far from this famous shopping location is Chennai's shoreline. Walking along the Bay of Bengal, part of the shore-line near her home on the eastern coast of Chennai, Deepti and her friends are taking a lunch break between classes. Just as they are about to enjoy a meal of daal and rice, packed carefully away in a tiffin box (a stackable metal lunch box popular in the region), they notice a sign along the waterfront. Featuring the graphic of a large blue wave, the sign warns people to leave the beach when there is a tsunami warning. It asks residents to listen for the sound of an alarm.

The warning brings back painful images for Deepti. She has vivid memories of the destruction caused by the Asian tsu-nami, caused by the great Sumatra-Andaman earthquake. On December 26, 2004, the tsunami hit this Indian shore, as well as coastal areas of the surrounding region. More than 225,000 people in 11 countries, including India, were killed.

Although saddened by the reminder provided by the sign, Deepti also appreciates the public education program that was funded, in part, by the World Bank and the International Monetary Fund (IMF), two international financial organiza-tions. In 2005, in response to the destruction caused by the Asian tsunami, the IMF contributed $158.4 million for emer-gency relief, disaster education, and for rebuilding India and other countries that suffered losses as a result of the tsunami.[1]

India is a developing country; 44.2 percent of the popula-tion lives on less than one dollar a day and the average annual income is $905. This average annual income is known as the

Here, a worker in a village in the Philippines puts up a sign that reads "Tsunami, This Way to Safe Area," in May 2006. Although the Philippines was not one of the 11 countries devastated by the 2004 tsunami that killed more than 225,000 residents along coasts bordering the Indian Ocean, the Philippines must still prepare for such natural disasters because of its Pacific Ocean location.

gross domestic product (GDP) per capita, or per person, which is a measure of a country's total output of goods and services. The United States is a high-income country, with an average annual income of $43,800.[2] A person living in the United States consumes twice as much grain, twice as much fish, three times as much meat, nine times as much paper, and eleven times as much gasoline as someone living in India.[3] Of course, poverty exists in the United States; however, when compared with less-developed countries, there are more social supports, including government and charitable programs, to assist individuals living at or below the poverty line in the United States.

How should the gap between developing and high-income countries be bridged? This gap poses a huge challenge for the World Bank and the IMF. With development and poverty reduction guiding the work that these global organizations do each day, the World Bank and the IMF are trying to meet the challenges of global inequalities.

The World Bank defines extreme poverty as living on less than one dollar a day. Moderate poverty is defined as living on less than two dollars a day.[4] For a typical teenager in the United States, by contrast, two dollars a day might be what one spends on a cup of coffee, a bottle of soda, a pack of gum, or two songs downloaded from the Internet.

Development is a process of positive growth for a country. As countries move from less developed to developed status, the availability of social and economic opportunities for citizens affects individuals, communities, and entire countries. These opportunities include health care, education, political participation, employment, and access to shelter, food, and clothing. Whether through direct intervention by organizations like the World Bank and the IMF, from donations by other countries, or with the assistance of nongovernmental organizations (NGOs) such as World Vision and CARE, development can—and, indeed, should—benefit the whole community. Once basic needs are met, people can begin to contribute to the growth of their communities and to the country by working, earning money, spending money, saving money, and providing employment and taxation revenues.

Accessible education is one important way the World Bank and the IMF are addressing poverty and promoting development. The World Bank is the world's largest supporter of education. As of 2005, the World Bank has provided $33 billion in loans and credits for education, benefiting 157 projects in 83 countries.[5]

Deepti's school, an institution for young women that was funded and built by contributions from the World Bank, is special to her. For Deepti, who is a strong student, school is a place of opportunity and growth. Her family wants her to get an education, and ongoing funding provided by the World Bank reduces the tuition costs her family must pay. Still, some of Deepti's friends cannot afford the tuition costs, and since greater priority is placed on the education of boys in her community, many girls do not complete school.

While walking back from her lunch break, Deepti notices some of the bank branches that line the main street of Chennai. To develop a strong banking system in India, the IMF has worked closely with the country. A strong banking system sends a positive signal to other countries; in this case, the message is that India is a country that other countries can invest in and trade with. Knowing that money is protected, other countries are more willing to work with India. As more investment arrives, growth increases. As a result, greater productivity and profits can be made by Indian companies and their workers. The joint partnership between the IMF and India has resulted in many benefits—price stability (prices for food staples and primary resources are predictable and protected from massive inflation); reduced inflation (as prices remain stable, people have more money to spend on consumer goods); and increased business development opportunities as a result of bank loans.

For example, the Indian information-technology sector benefits greatly from the investment and support offered by the World Bank and the IMF. Two of India's important exports are the central processing units (CPUs) and memory cards found in many computers. Thanks to investment by the World Bank and the IMF, Indian information-technology companies (the companies that develop and manufacture computers and related equipment) have grown. In part, this is due to the development of computer software and engineering programs in high schools and colleges in India. Using a community-based Internet access point, Deepti can check the latest trends, read news stories, or even submit a passport application. With travel and world issues being two of her interests, Deepti hopes to visit the United States to see the headquarters of the World Bank and the IMF in Washington, D.C.

Yet, many people are unable to access this technology, in spite of the numerous computer engineers, information-technology manufacturing plants, and call centers in the country, because it is not affordable. There is a digital divide between those who can and cannot access computer technology. For example, nearly 70 percent of North Americans use the Internet on a daily basis. By contrast, that figure is estimated to be less than 7 percent in Asia and 2 percent in Africa.[6]

"Our Dream Is a World Free of Poverty" is written on a banner that hangs in the lobby of the World Bank. Thousands of miles away from Deepti's home in India, these words link the work of the World Bank and the IMF to the realities and lives of young people like Deepti. Deepti is just one of the 1.1 billion 15- to 24-year-olds in the world inheriting a planet with big gaps between the rich and the poor. One hundred thirty-three million young people do not know how to read or write; half of all HIV infections occur among individuals aged 15 to 24 years old; every day 34,000 children die from hunger and related causes; 74 million youth are currently without work, representing 47 percent of the world's total unemployment; and, since 1987, 2 million

An *infothela* ("info-cart") is a mobile Internet classroom that provides computer technology in places where modern equipment is not available in rural India. The three-wheeled rickshaw aims to improve education, health care, and access to agricultural information by using fax, Internet, and telephone service and by moving between village clusters situated approximately one to three miles apart. These school children gather around an infothela in the village of Bithoor in India.

children have been killed, 6 million have been disabled, and 12 million made homeless as a result of war.[7] Despite these figures, young people represent the future of growth and opportunity.

Aware of the challenges facing youth around the world, the World Bank and the IMF want to promote access to education, employment, conflict resolution, public health issues, and personal and community safety. In response, these organizations have created children-focused and youth-focused programs.

The World Bank's Children and Youth Framework for Action seeks to engage the voices and experiences of young people from around the world by consulting with youth, governments, and community-based organizations. In 2002, the World Bank established the Children and Youth Unit and in September 2003, the World Bank held the Youth, Development, and Peace conference in Paris, France. One hundred representatives from 70 countries identified youth's major concerns: employment, education, conflict resolution, and post-conflict rebuilding.

In September 2004 in Sarajevo, Bosnia and Herzegovina, a second conference repeated in even stronger terms the need for education, employment, conflict resolution, and rebuilding to be addressed by the World Bank. One young participant captures the frustration and hopes of all of the young people gathered together at the conferences:

> Millions of young people have had their dreams stolen. Yes, dreams! We human beings have to be fed, need air, a home, etc., but more than that, we have to be able to dream . . . because surviving does not equal living, and to live is to be able to grow, to hope, to create, and to plan.[8]

In response to the needs identified by the conference participants, the World Bank created the Youth Voices project. Selected via an application process, young people were given the opportunity to volunteer in the World Bank's offices in their home countries. In addition to researching topics as diverse as access to education and gender equality, the young people were invited to share their advice and responses to World Bank policies. The program proved so successful that Youth Voices groups now operate in Bosnia, Brazil, Egypt, Ethiopia, Kenya, Kosovo, Macedonia, Moldova, Turkey, and Yemen.[9]

Poverty cannot be addressed without looking at not only the local, but also the global symptoms, causes, and solutions.

One cannot enjoy and exercise her or his full global citizenship without seeing one's connections to self and others. Whether it is Deepti's experiences or one's own, there is a commonality of experiences that may offer solutions to pressing global issues, including poverty reduction and development promotion. Forming part of a global community, we are all connected. The local informs the global, and vice versa.

Compelling in its appeal to the "global village" and the dialogue between cultures, globalization questions and influences the measures of development and standards of living for billions of people worldwide. Former Secretary-General of the United Nations Kofi Annan's support of globalization captures the desire to achieve sustainability and improve the lives of the world's people. He observed:

> Globalization offers great opportunities, but at present, its benefits are very unevenly distributed while its costs are borne by all.... Some people fear that globalization makes inequality worse. The relationship between the two is complex. With the exception of the economies in transition, recent increases in income gaps are largely the result of technological changes that favor higher skilled workers over less skilled ones. As the economic benefits of education and skills increase, so does income inequality between the people who have them and those who do not.... Globalization may exacerbate these differences, but it does not cause them. Increased global competition may also restrain income gains in relatively higher wage countries, though to date this effect has been felt mainly in the industrialized countries.[10]

Negotiation within organizations like the World Bank and the IMF offers the possibility to reconsider the us-versus-them thinking—protestor versus trade negotiator—associated with globalization. Even if there is agreement on the predominant influences and historical unfolding of globalization, a precise definition remains elusive. Annan continued:

> [W]e need to be very specific with regard to what we mean by "globalization." One of the major errors made when discussing globalization today is that its meaning is often obscure, with different people using it to denote different processes, and with very different—and sometimes emotional—connotations. In this sense, trying to grapple with the concept of globalization becomes somewhat akin to a skirmish with a shadow. To overcome this state, which more often than not inhibits a factual and pragmatic discussion of globalization, we need to focus on the multi-dimensional character of globalization, or in other words to break it down into its constituent elements.[11]

Hans van Ginkel, the rector of United Nations University (UNU), a research center associated with the United Nations, argues that the goals of poverty reduction and development promotion must be interconnected on the local, national, and global levels. For economic and social benefits to happen, all of us, no matter where we live, must work together to achieve these goals.

Deepti's life and experiences, while geographically far from the United States, are not disconnected from our own local life and global awareness.

Introduction to the World Bank and the International Monetary Fund

THE WORLD BANK AND THE INTERNATIONAL MONETARY FUND (IMF), often confused with each other, were both founded on July 1, 1944. Because they were created in Bretton Woods, New Hampshire, they are referred to as the Bretton Woods institutions. Sharing a common founding moment after the Great Depression and at the end of World War II, the World Bank and the IMF are distinct organizations with the shared goals of poverty reduction and development promotion. The World Bank was originally known as the International Bank for Reconstruction and Development (IBRD). A journalist thought that name was too long and difficult to remember, so he referred to the IBRD as the World Bank and this new name stuck. In 1975, the World Bank became the official title.

Originally composed of 45 member nations, the IMF wanted to avoid the conditions that led to the Great Depression (1929–1939) and the destruction following World War II (1939–1945). The post-World War II period is significant in terms of the growth of the Bretton Woods institutions. Specifically, the Marshall Plan would help to forge a more united Western Europe after the losses of World War II. Officially called the European Recovery Program, the Marshall Plan, named for then-secretary of state George Marshall, was established on July 12, 1947. Operating between 1947 and 1952, the Marshall Plan expended $13 billion to assist with the economic and technical rebuilding of Western Europe. All Western European countries, with the exception of Spain (which was controlled by General Francisco Franco) participated.

The Bretton Woods institutions looked to the Marshall Plan as a model of economic coordination, financial growth, and economic stability, in addition to positioning the United States as a leading international actor after World War II. The Marshall Plan was significant in terms of its ability to end protective trade barriers, stimulate trade between Europe and the United States, and coordinate economic growth across Europe. The Marshall Plan also marks one of the key divisions that would lead to the Cold War (the Soviet Union was opposed to American economic influence).

Through a shared commitment to economic cooperation and an ongoing desire to promote global growth and economic stability after World War II, the IMF committed itself to ensuring the strength of the world's monetary and financial systems (the companies and organizations dealing with money and banking, including banks, stock markets, insurance companies, and government departments). These systems oversee international payment processes between countries and the exchange rates of different national currencies.

Today, the World Bank employs 10,000 people. Of that number, 7,000 are based at the World Bank headquarters in Washington, D.C. The other 3,000 employees are located around the world in 100 World Bank field offices.[12] The experts on staff bring relevant skills, knowledge, and experiences to the World Bank. They include economists who study the market, the number of imports and exports, employment rates, and the overall economic well-being of a country; engineers who provide technical expertise to support projects as diverse as building roads, waterways, water filtration plants, schools, homes, and other public buildings; public policy experts who examine government policies to ensure these support the development, growth, and well-being of a country; and social scientists trained in fields such as sociology and anthropology who see whether the results of policies actually promote positive change. Experts examine World Bank and IMF policies in terms of particular social concerns, including gender equality and environmental sustainability. For example, if the World Bank and IMF direct money and resources to build schools in a region, but if there is a gender bias held by the citizens that says girls should not go to school, then the school-building program will not benefit half of the population. A gender equality expert could help to avoid this problem by working with, listening to, and learning from the community to develop girl-friendly schools.

The World Bank and the IMF are specialized, but independent, agencies affiliated with the United Nations (UN). The UN and its member agencies, including such well-known ones as the United Nations Children's Fund (UNICEF) and the World Health Organization (WHO), work with the World Bank and the IMF to identify shared issues of concern and to develop programs and coordinate responses to development and poverty reduction. The World Bank focuses on long-term economic development and poverty reduction. It provides the funds and technical knowledge needed to create and support programs that will make a positive difference in people's lives. For example, the World Bank contributed some of the money and engineering knowledge necessary to rebuild the social infrastructure—the roads, hospitals, homes, schools, and sanitation facilities— needed by the countries affected by the 2004 Asian Tsunami.

World Bank Organization Chart

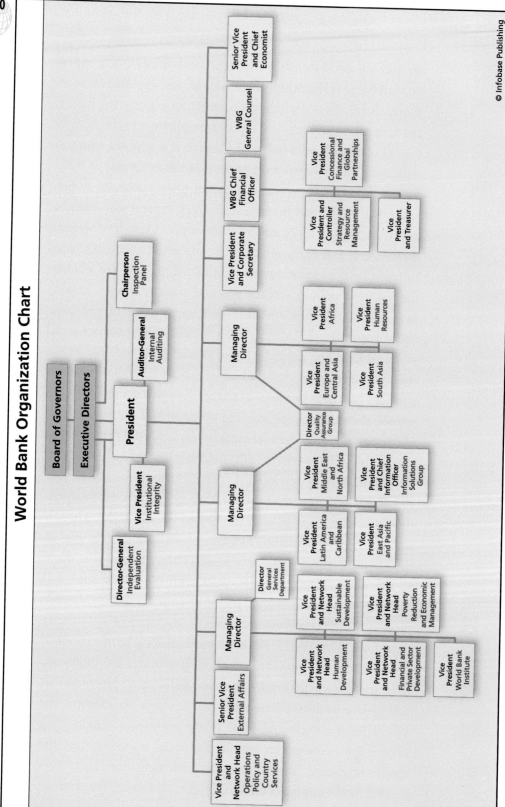

The IMF attempts to ensure the stability of national and international financial systems. A country's financial (monetary) system includes its banks, stock markets, pension funds, insurance companies and services, and central bank. The central bank, also known as a reserve bank or monetary authority, oversees the monetary system of a country or block of countries. In the United States, the U.S. Federal Reserve Department, part of the U.S. Treasury Department, is responsible for responding to global economic trends, setting interest rates, stabilizing the national currency, and producing and circulating money. The central bank can also loan money to banks to avert a financial crisis.

Between 2006 and 2008, for example, selected American banks received federal funds after a large segment of their clients defaulted on mortgages (a type of loan used to purchase a home). Having been offered mortgages with interest rates lower than the average rate charged by their banks, called variable rate mortgages, many consumers purchased homes with little or no down payment required. Unfortunately, many consumers faced daunting financial challenges: high levels of personal consumer debt, especially credit card debt; low salaries that prevented consumers from paying their debts; job losses in such economic sectors as technology and manufacturing; and higher interest rates on mortgages. Many home buyers were unable to pay their monthly mortgages. As a result, the banks foreclosed (when a bank or other creditor repossesses a property) on the homes.

In addition to people being without homes, the banks also suffered big financial losses since the loans could not be repaid. In response, many banks turned to the central bank for financial

(Opposite page) When the World Bank was first established on July 1, 1944, aid was provided chiefly to European countries for the reconstruction of industries destroyed during World War II. Since the late 1960s, loans have been granted to projects that could directly benefit the poorest people in developing nations in Africa, Asia, and Latin America.

assistance. As a demonstration of global interconnections, it is interesting to note that in response to the financial challenges in the United States, growth in East Asia will decline to 8.5 percent in 2008, a projected one to two percent decline for the year.[13]

The IMF seeks to expand international trade between countries. It takes the view that trade is good for countries since it is a source of income. When foreign countries buy goods produced in the United States, for instance, these overseas purchases generate income and jobs in the United States. If the demand for products is great, then the industry makes more money. In turn, as supply increases, there will be more jobs available in U.S. communities. When citizens are employed and earning wages, they spend this money on goods and services. Purchases include homes, investment products—stocks, bonds, and treasury bills—cars, clothing, and vacations. As a result of increased jobs, investment, and opportunities, the entire community benefits.

Drawn to a developing country by its lower wages, stable economy, and well-educated work force, a U.S. computer company might decide to invest in technical support call centers in India. By investing in the community, the computer company provides jobs, additional training, and income. In turn, employees can use their income to help pay tuition, contribute to their families' well-being, save and invest money with their local banks, and buy products from community-based businesses. This process is known as investment. As companies and governments invest time and money, and new and existing industries expand, increased employment results.

(opposite page) **With the exceptions of North Korea, Cuba, Andorra, Monaco, Liechtenstein, Tuvalu, and Nauru, all UN members participate in the IMF. It is an organization of 185 countries that works to promote global monetary cooperation, secure financial stability, facilitate international trade, promote high employment and sustainable economic growth, and reduce poverty.**

International Monetary Fund Organization Chart

International Monetary and Financial Commitee

Board of Governors

Joint IMF–World Bank Development Committee*

Executive Board

Independent Evaluation Office

Managing Director
Deputy Managing Directors

Investment Office–Staff Retirement Plan

Office of Budget and Planning

Office of Internal Audit and Inspection

Office of Technical Assistance Management

Area Departments

African Department

Asia and Pacific Department

Regional Office for Asia and the Pacific

European Department

Offices in Europe

Middle East and Central Asia Department

Western Hemisphere Department

Functional and Special Services Departments

Finance Department

Legal Department

Fiscal Affairs Department

Monetary and Capital Markets Department

IMF Institute

Policy Development and Review Department

Joint Africa Institute

Joint Vienna Institute

Singapore Training Institute

Research Department

Statistics Department

Information and Liaison

External Relations Department

Fund Office United Nations**

Support Services

Human Resources Department

Secretary's Department

Technology and General Services Department

* Known formally as the Joint Ministerial Committee of the Boards of Governors of the Bank and the Fund on the Transfer of Real Resources to Developing Countries.

** Attached to the Office of the Managing Director.

© Infobase Publishing

23

However, there are limitations to this economic growth. For instance, as the United States looks to international markets to supply cheaper products, these imports decrease the incentives and ability of local communities to produce their own goods. In turn, the importation of these foreign goods reduces opportunities for local industrial and job growth in the United States.

The IMF also promotes exchange rate stability. For example, when people or companies trade U.S. dollars at the bank for the European euro, Japanese yen, or British pound, there will not be too much difference in price from bank to bank. Price stability—prices staying the same—is important for trade. Companies buying and selling products want to know how much things will cost. If the value of the currency changes too much, then trade will suffer. Some computer central processing units are made in India but imported by United States companies. Importers, including those large American computer companies, have to be able to estimate how much the CPUs will cost. They do not want the price to go up too much from day to day.

Today, the IMF has 185 member countries, including the United States. Its 2,635 staff members come from 143 countries. Each member state may send one representative to serve on the board of governors, which meets once a year. Of this group, 24 governors sit on the International Monetary and Finance Committee. This committee meets twice a year to discuss the IMF's projects. Daily operations are overseen from the Washington, D.C., headquarters.

UNDERSTANDING DEVELOPMENT

The World Bank and the IMF work to promote development. Development is a process of positive change in poorer countries that results in improved livelihoods and a better quality of life. Economist Amartya Sen argues that people cannot exercise their full human rights without a dignified standard of living.[14] Development as freedom, an idea proposed by Sen, is the idea that people cannot be free unless their basic needs, including food, clothing, health care, and shelter, are met. Once these needs are met, citizens can then assume more active roles within the political system. For instance, if a parent has sufficient food, clean drinking water, shelter, and clothing, and health care for herself and her children—the basic necessities of life—then she can devote more time and energy to becoming aware of the larger social and political issues affecting her community and country, including access to education for her children and fighting gender discrimination against her daughters. As people reduce poverty, they participate in making rules for their own countries, regions, and villages; find ways of meeting their basic human needs and living with dignity; and make their communities more cohesive and interesting.

As a development institution, the World Bank provides the money and information needed by countries that may be having a difficult time meeting the basic needs of their populations. The IMF, also a development institution, is a cooperative financial institution dedicated to stabilizing the international monetary system, including currency rates and payments between countries. By doing so, the IMF helps to foster development.

However, the development process can be controversial, too. If a developing country comes to rely upon donations from the World Bank, the IMF, or developed countries, then this creates a relationship of dependence. Another concern is the extent to which the World Bank and the IMF direct national policies.

THE GOALS OF THE WORLD BANK

The World Bank is an investment bank. It works to achieve the central goals of supporting the development of impoverished countries and reducing poverty. Unlike a local bank branch, which works with individual customers and businesses, the

World Bank invests money and other resources, including technical and economic knowledge, in entire countries and big projects. These include education and health care for billions of people around the world.

With the main goals of reducing poverty and fostering development, the World Bank Group (WBG) consists of five member organizations.

- The International Bank for Reconstruction and Development (IBRD) provides development assistance, including loans and grants, to middle-income countries in Asia, eastern Europe, Latin America, and Africa.
- The International Development Association (IDA) provides development assistance, including loans and grants, to the poorest countries around the world.
- The International Financial Corporation (IFC) provides money and other financial expertise to encourage private investments (money put into a business or economy by private companies, not by governments) in developing countries. This expertise includes economic modeling (a way to predict economic outcomes, often via mathematics) about the impacts of monetary policy in the country. Monetary policy, as determined by a country's central bank, refers to the ability to control the supply and availability of money in circulation to achieve low unemployment, low inflation, and economic growth.
- The Multilateral Investment Guarantee Agency (MIGA) promises to protect investments in these developing regions. For example, if a company invests one million dollars in a developing country but then loses its original investment, the MIGA will repay the company the money it has lost. Investments can be lost for a variety of reasons. These include poor financial planning, loss of interest in the product being sold, misuse of funds,

or recession (a downturn in the economy causing people to have less money to spend, higher unemployment, and reduced demand for products).

- The International Center for Settlement of Investment Disputes (ICSID) resolves disputes between foreign investors and host countries. For instance, a conflict might arise when a foreign investor seeks repayment of a loan, but the country or an individual business is slow to repay. The ICSID mediates by trying to find a solution that is acceptable to both parties. The World Bank, run cooperatively, borrows money from some member countries and lends to other member countries.

The United States is the largest donor country because it has the biggest economy in the world. Member countries receive shares of the votes on the World Bank's policies and programs. The United States has the largest share of the votes with 16.4 percent.[15] This means that the United States controls 16.4 percent of the spending and decision-making power of the World Bank. Japan has 7.9 percent, Germany has 4.5 percent, the United Kingdom has 4.3 percent, and France has 4.3 percent. Each member country may send one representative to serve as part of the World Bank.

As of 2007, the board of the World Bank has approved $22.3 billion in loans and grants to support 278 projects around the globe.[16]

Aside from the funds provided by individual governments, the World Bank is the largest source of money for education. The World Bank is also one of the largest supporters of HIV and AIDS awareness, treatment, and prevention programs; biodiversity (having various types of plants and trees); and the provision of clean water, electricity, and transportation.

The World Bank opposes the misuse of funds by member countries and individuals. This misuse can occur through theft (governments or government officials stealing money from

World Bank or the IMF loans or grants) or the inappropriate use of the funds. For example, a country could promise to use the money to build schools, but instead spend the money on another—and unapproved—purpose.

Unlike private banks, the World Bank does not try to make a profit on its products and services. It usually charges a low interest rate of 0.5 percent. (The IMF charges higher interest rates on some of its loans.)

THE GOALS OF THE INTERNATIONAL MONETARY FUND

The IMF seeks to promote cooperation among countries in banking, stock markets, trade, and investments. The IMF does this by providing funds and expertise about money-related systems (for example, banks, stock markets, and ministries of finance) to make cooperation possible. It also facilitates the expansion and balanced growth of international trade (trade between two or more countries) in the hopes that this growth will result in high levels of employment and living wages. A living wage enables workers to earn enough money with which to live, meet more than their basic necessities, plan, and save money. The IMF promotes international exchange stability. This is a predictable rate of exchange when buying or selling one currency for another.

In addition, the IMF helps countries with their balance of payments. The balance of payments refers to all of the money coming in and going out of a country, from the payments and receipts from the transactions of residents and businesses in one country to other countries. Incoming funds are known as credits; outgoing funds are known as debits. These credits and debits include all of the consumer purchases, imports, and exports in that country. When a country has a large number of payments, this is known as a surplus. A surplus is like having more funds in your bank account than you spend. A surplus is beneficial for a country. Excess funds provide economic stability and a source of growth. With these surplus funds a country can provide tax incentives to individuals and companies, fund infrastructure projects like roads and public transportation, and invest in economic sectors like technology and health research. The IMF seeks to reduce the amount and number of payments to achieve a balanced or surplus balance of payments.

GOALS SHARED BY THE
WORLD BANK AND THE IMF

The World Bank and the IMF support debt relief for countries unable to repay large loans. Debt relief is like loan forgiveness. As an illustration, students who go to college often get loans to pay for their college tuition and fees. If instead of requiring students to repay their loans after they graduated from college banks did not require payment, they would be "forgiving" the loan. Instead of having to work hard to pay back the thousands of dollars, a former student would owe nothing and be able to use all of her income to pay for housing, food, and transportation. Debt relief is similar, except it applies to countries that have borrowed billions of dollars from an organization like the World Bank or the IMF. Even with debt forgiveness, some countries are still having a difficult time making the basic necessities of life available to all of their citizens.

The World Bank and the IMF are committed to supporting the development of countries around the world. A poor country could approach the World Bank to ask for loans, grants, and technical support. Working cooperatively with the World Bank, the country identifies areas of greatest need, such as access to health care and education, reducing illiteracy, providing enough nutritious food and safe drinking water, and building safe roads. The World Bank provides information about environmental protection programs like recycling and getting fuel from alternative sources like the sun, water, and wind and it sponsors public awareness campaigns to promote healthier

In 2000, at the 13th International AIDS Conference in South Africa, AIDS activists called for debt relief to poor countries, which would make cheaper drugs available. In 2005, in one of the biggest write-offs ever, finance ministers from the eight richest nations agreed to cancel $40 billion in debt held by the world's poorest nations. Eighteen nations in all, 14 of them in Africa, had their debts erased and were allowed to apply for new loans, with the promise to use funds on free primary education, improved health care, infrastructure construction, and agriculture development.

lifestyle choices to reduce the spread of HIV/AIDS and other diseases. The country could then develop programs and receive technical support. This support could include medical and educational training for doctors, nurses, and teachers, building schools, providing support for farmers, and offering medical assistance to pregnant women and families.

Even if the World Bank and the IMF provide financial and technical support, there are no guarantees that a country's problems will end, poverty will cease, and development will benefit all of its citizens. In addition to whether poverty and underdevelopment can be addressed on a wide scale, other controversial questions remain about the extent to which the World Bank and the IMF enable dependence and underdevelopment, compromise national control, or impose Western ideas upon non-Western environments.

MEMBERSHIP AND QUOTAS

The World Bank and the IMF are funded by its member countries. Each member country provides financial contributions, known as quotas, which are tied to the size of the country and its economy. These contributions vary from nation to nation. The more quotas received, the more money the IMF is able to provide in loans. As of July 2006, the IMF had quotas totaling $317 billion.[17] Since it has the largest economy in the world, the United States has the biggest quota at the IMF. It is also the most powerful member country.

Countries, unable to go to a local bank branch the way individuals can, work with the IMF and request loans. As of 2006, the IMF had loaned $28 billion to 74 countries. In addition to money, the IMF provides monetary policy and technical assistance on financial matters. This technical assistance includes how to build and maintain national banking systems, monetary policy, and fiscal policy. Monetary policy, overseen by a country's central bank, determines the availability of currency, interest rates, and currency stability. Fiscal policy refers to the government's budgetary policy. Reviewing the amount of government spending versus tax revenues derived from taxes, fiscal policy considers the approach a government should take to foster economic growth.

As a country's financial system strengthens, it may use this knowledge and increased funding, from foreign investment, economic growth, and the IMF loans and grants, to help it support a wide range of social programs. In 2006, the IMF provided the equivalent of 429.9 persons years of technical

assistance. This support allows countries to make good decisions about how the loan will be spent so it may benefit the
most people.

Private banks enable people and businesses to apply for
loans, pay bills, purchase bonds and certificates of investment
(also known as CIs—an investor provides the bank with a
sum of money and gets an interest payment over a period of
time, usually one year or longer), open checking and savings
accounts, get a mortgage, secure a loan to help pay for tuition,
obtain a credit card, and allow a person or business to exchange
American dollars into foreign currencies, whether you are
buying and selling products with another country or if you are
planning a trip outside of the United States. People with vary-
ing degrees of wealth can use a wide range of products and
services. Banks give people advice about how to use money
wisely. This advice comes in many forms: information and
products that allow people to invest money in the stock market
and bonds, plan for retirement, budget, and protect themselves
from financial fraud and identity theft.

Like individuals, countries may also need assistance with
financial matters. The World Bank and the IMF provide
assistance to countries, particularly the poorest countries that
are home to the 1.3 billion people who live on less than the
equivalent of one dollar a day.[18] Their assistance contributes to
various projects, including initiatives to provide clean drinking
water, increase awareness of and reduce the stigma surrounding the human immunodeficiency virus (HIV) and acquired
immunodeficiency syndrome (AIDS), and offer primary education to young people.

UNDERSTANDING THE LOAN PROCESS: COMPARING HOW AN INDIVIDUAL VERSUS A COUNTRY GETS A LOAN

The IMF works with individual countries, just like banks or
credit card companies work with individual customers, to

develop a realistic debt repayment plan. The IMF looks carefully at loan applications. It requires a sound plan for using the money. The IMF reviews a country's policies, programs, and financial statements when considering a loan application. The IMF examines the progress of its projects through a process called surveillance consultations. The IMF checks in on these countries to see how the funds are being used. As of 2006, 128 countries have received surveillance consultations.[19]

DEVELOPMENT IN ACTION: ACCESS TO EDUCATION AND THE MILLENNIUM DEVELOPMENT GOALS

In September 2000, the United Nations created a detailed framework to promote and achieve development in the form of eight Millennium Development Goals (MDGs). These MDGs seek to achieve the following: eradicate extreme poverty and hunger; promote gender equality and women's empowerment; reduce child mortality; improve maternal health; combat HIV/AIDS, malaria, and other diseases; ensure environmental sustainability; develop a global partnership for development; and achieve universal primary education.

The MDGs pose massive challenges for the World Bank and the IMF. For example, the access to education goal will cost between $9.1 billion and $38 billion each year between 2006 and 2015. Most of this money must come from developing countries. Since they are poor, these countries by themselves will not be able to come up with the estimated $5 billion to $7 billion each country needs to achieve this goal. Other sources of funding will have to provide this money.[20]

Since it started lending money for education in 1963, to date, the World Bank has transferred more than $40 billion in loans and credits to low- and middle-income countries. In 2007, education lending reached $2 billion. The World Bank also approved 28 educational projects in 2007. Two of the largest projects provided $280 million for vocational and technical

Female empowerment and equality have been identified by the World Bank, the IMF, and nongovernmental organizations as key aspects to sustainable development in poor communities. The first action is attracting workers that can alter views on long-standing traditional values (such as dowries, child labor, and submissive roles given to women in families). These young women, above, from the Kibera area in Nairobi, Kenya, are taking self-empowerment classes to learn about their bodies, their right to say no, safe sex education, and financial empowerment through savings.

education in India and $250 million for accessible primary schools in Nigeria.[21]

In 2002, the World Bank introduced the Education for All Fast Track Initiative (FTI). Benin, Cambodia, Mali, Mauritania, Mongolia, Mozambique, and Sierra Leone—seven low-income countries in Africa and Asia—received $265 million in grant supports. With focused funding provided to these countries, and the countries themselves showing strong education plans, the FTI has been successful in its efforts to increase access to education. Focused funding means that all of the agencies, including the government, NGOs, World Bank, and the IMF, work together to maximize their spending to see positive results.

Although it might be safe to assume that education is—and should be—available to all youth, it is not. Financial and cultural pressures can affect who gets to attend school in some developing countries. These pressures include the need to have children work to earn income to support the family, lack of cultural and financial support for further education, and the cultural view that the education of boys is more important than the education of girls.

Considering this last barrier to education, how is the gender inequality in education best addressed? Money can be a strong and effective motivator. More than 150,000 poor girls in Punjab, Pakistan in grades six to eight receive funds to encourage them to stay in school. Similarly, the Bolsa Familia Project in Brazil provides families with money to educate their children. Girls and boys, aged 7 to 15 years, must be in school to receive funding. Low-income Mexican families receive money only if they ensure their children go to school and visit medical clinics. This funding program is also at work in other countries, including Yemen and Chad. The number of primary school-aged children out of school has fallen from 100 million in 2000 to an estimated 77 million in 2006. As more girls attend school, the ratio of girls to boys in school is also increasing.[22]

In the West African country of Burkina Faso the International Development Association (IDA), part of the World Bank Group, introduced additional funds, from $32.6 million to $110 million, in support of basic education. Coordination of support from funding partners—including Belgium, Canada, Denmark, the European Commission, France, the Netherlands, Sweden, UNICEF, and nongovernmental organizations—increased the

(continues on page 38)

A DAY IN THE LIFE OF A WORLD BANK SECTORAL EXPERT

Originally from Tehran, Ladan[*] became interested in gender equality—treating women and men fairly and equally—while growing up in Iran. Just 16 years old at the time of the Iranian revolution in 1979, she saw her country change before her eyes. Iran went from having a monarchy led by the Shah of Iran to an Islamic republic under the leadership of the Ayatollah Ruhollah Khomeini. Women had to wear more modest coverings, and unless they were with immediate relatives, women and girls were often segregated in public places from boys and men. Of greatest concern to Ladan, though, was the denial of full legal and civil rights to women. For example, a woman testifying in court did not have the same authority as a man. Women did not have the same right of inheritance as men. While a man could have as many as four wives, a woman could have only one husband.

Ladan's family made the difficult decision to leave Iran. The family went to the United States to start a new life in 1980, settling in Los Angeles. Los Angeles is home to one of the largest Iranian—or Persian—communities in the world outside of Iran. Although you will not find the country of Persia on any contemporary world map, it is a term many Iranians use to refer to themselves, their language, and their culture.

After earning her bachelor of arts and master of arts degrees in international affairs, she completed an unpaid internship at the World Bank headquarters.

---

* Like all of the composite profiles of professionals associated with the World Bank and the IMF profiled in this text, Ladan is not an actual person; however, Ladan is a composite of actual workers, experiences, roles, and knowledge associated with the World Bank and the IMF.

Today, Ladan is a gender equality expert. On a typical day she will begin by checking her e-mail. She receives between 100 and 200 e-mails each day. There could be messages about program and policy development at the World Bank, press releases and reports from nongovernmental and governmental organizations, invitations to panel discussions and book launches, and status reports about the Millennium Development Goals.

After replying to the most urgent e-mails, Ladan meets with the team of gender equality experts. Together, they determine priorities for the week or month ahead, provide reports about their work, and brainstorm to resolve issues. Next, Ladan carefully reads all of the program and policy drafts the World Bank is developing. She looks at these policies and programs with one question in mind: How does this policy or program support gender equality? She completes written reports outlining ways to enhance gender equality. These reports are shared with the director.

Ladan also works with partners, including government representatives, nongovernmental organization (NGO) representatives, and sectoral experts in other fields, to share ideas and develop action plans. Amnesty International, Human Rights Watch, and Doctors Without Borders are examples of NGOs interested in promoting gender equality through human rights. NGOs are citizen-led organizations, separate from the government, that promote political issues or social causes.

Although the work is intellectually challenging, detail-oriented, and time-consuming, Ladan is proud of the contributions she is making. She also sees her work with the World Bank as an extension of the original activism and questions she had as a teenager.

(continued from page 35)
number of schools in Burkina Faso by 550,000. Overall enrollment rates have increased to 62 percent (55 percent for girls) in
2006. This represents an increase of 20 percent, from 42 percent
(36 percent for girls) in 2000. In the lowest income provinces in
Burkina Faso, enrollment increased to 47 percent (41 percent for
girls). This is an increase of 17 percent, from 30 percent (24 percent for girls) between the years 2000 and 2006. Looking ahead
to secondary education, a similar program is in development.[23]

MAKING GLOBAL CONNECTIONS
THROUGH THE WORLD BANK AND THE IMF

Citizens of wealthier countries are indirect members of the
World Bank and the IMF by contributing to their own country's growth and development and by participating in setting
their own country's political direction. Looking beyond the
daily operations of these organizations, one sees global institutions that weave together a shared sense of connectivity.

As a result of their strong economies, the largest contribu-
tors and most powerful members of the World Bank and the
IMF, notably the United States, France, Germany, and Japan,
are influencing the MDGs and development processes in
poorer countries. Critics have also raised concerns about the
degree to which the World Bank and the IMF interfere with
national economies and sovereignty (a country's ability to be
autonomous and make its own decisions).

2

The History of the World Bank and the International Monetary Fund

As we read in Chapter 1, the World Bank and the IMF were first suggested at a United Nations conference in Bretton Woods, New Hampshire, in July 1944. Later, in 1945, the IMF was officially created to promote global growth and economic stability. The 45 governments that attended the first conference wanted to ensure economic cooperation. They did not want to repeat the Great Depression and thought that careful economic planning and cooperation might avoid a recurrence. In addition, they recognized the need to rebuild Europe after the devastation of World War II.

The Depression was a worldwide economic downtown that affected all segments of the economy. Job losses, factory closures, personal and business bankruptcies, lack of food, homelessness, and widespread personal despair characterized

Many factors contributed to the Great Depression (1929–1939), including the uneven distribution of wealth, the introduction of credit ("buy now, pay later"), and the large number of less-affluent investors who borrowed money to buy large shares of stock. In the summer of 1929, the United States experienced an economic downturn, and the stock market crashed due to investors selling all of their stocks, resulting in losses estimated at $30 billion by mid-November. Here, panicked crowds pack the Wall Street district in New York City on October 24, 1929, also known as Black Tuesday.

this era. On October 29, 1929, also called Black Tuesday, the New York stock market crashed. Stock prices fell sharply, causing most investors to lose their investments.

The decade (1920–1929) prior to the Depression was known as the Roaring Twenties. In this prosperous period, paper money flowed freely and families used credit to purchase goods and services, including food, clothing, housing, and health services. Many people also purchased investments "on margin." Buying on margin, or in installments, people paid only a small fraction of the actual cost of an investment, promising to pay the rest of the cost later to a bank or lending company. The investor had to promise to repay the outstanding total balance at the time of purchase, even if the actual value of the stock or goods declined and even if they were out of money. As more and more people purchased stocks on margin, stocks lost their value and investors lost their ability to pay what they owed. These factors led to the stock market crash.

Black Tuesday had very serious consequences. International trade declined rapidly, as companies found themselves unable to afford imports. Construction slowed because companies did not have the funds necessary to build and renovate buildings. Personal incomes fell as companies closed or laid off workers. Tax revenues declined since workers and the unemployed did not have the money to pay taxes. Without tax dollars, the government lost an important source of revenue. Crop prices in the American Midwest fell sharply. Demand for crops like wheat and corn fell, and individual shoppers reduced their spending on all products, including grocery staples like bread. There were many unemployed workers without enough food, clothing, or even housing. Unable to pay the rent, many people were forced out of their homes.

An unfortunate natural coincidence compounded the problems of the Great Depression. A big drought and accompanying winds created "dust bowls" (strong winds that dispersed seeds, preventing them from taking root in dry soil), in the Great Plains states. In the dry conditions, seeds were denied the water necessary for growth. Unable to take root in the dry soil conditions, the seeds blew away in the wind. Many farmers in the United States, responding to strong demand for certain crops, including wheat and corn, had become overly dependent upon producing these primary crops. As demand fell, coupled with the droughts and dust bowls, many farms had to close.

THE HUMAN FACE OF THE GREAT DEPRESSION

Originally raised in the small farming community of Holton, south of Omaha, Nebraska, Robert Jonas[24] never imagined he would be homeless. Life was not supposed to be like this for a successful farmer. Unfortunately, the Great Depression swallowed him and his family up into something bigger than they could have imagined.

Like many of his friends and neighbors, Robert was descended from a long line of farmers. In fact, his great-grandparents were among the last wave of homesteaders to settle in the region. Living in a state closely associated with cattle and crops, especially corn and wheat, Robert had the blood of farming running through his veins. He loved the open spaces, big sky, and daily challenge of working with nature. But nature and economics began to work against Robert.

A drought in 1925 marked the first sign of trouble for Robert and his farm. Unable to water his crop sufficiently, he experienced huge losses that year. These losses were compounded by fierce winds that prevented his seeds from taking root. Unable to pay his creditors, including the bank that loaned him money to purchase the additional farmland he had added to his property in 1928, he declared bankruptcy. Many of his family members and neighbors were experiencing similar losses. Unable to approach them for assistance, Robert could not face the reality that he would have to leave his beloved farm.

Likening the loss of the farm to a broken heart, he walked away from Holton. Seeing the many rail lines that crisscrossed the state, he became a drifter. With no security guards to stop him (many of them they had been laid off), he decided to ride the rails. Jumping into open freight cars, he moved from city to

After the U.S. Civil War, hopping freight trains became a common way of getting around, as railways began to expand westward. During the Great Depression, it was especially common among the poor who were unable to afford other transportation, and train hoppers became known as hobos. Today, the practice of freight hopping is forbidden in nearly every state.

city, state to state. Robert hopped off to look for casual work. From assembling boxes to yard work to ditch digging, Robert did all kinds of jobs. Stopping occasionally, Robert set up a temporary home, one made of cardboard boxes, in the makeshift communities that sprung up around rail yards throughout the United States.

As prosperity returned to the United States following World War II, Robert was able to return to his beloved farming in Nebraska; however, it would take several years of hard work before he could purchase a piece of farmland to call his own once again. He is but one of many faces and life stories from the Great Depression.

AFTER THE GREAT DEPRESSION

Seeking to protect their own industries and economies, many countries started to impose tariffs (taxes) upon foreign goods. Increased tariffs reduced the demand for exports from the United States, compounding the problem of depressed demand for goods. Many employees were laid off because their employers were unable to pay them. With little market demand for goods and services, companies closed. The Great Depression provided a powerful lesson about the need for good economic planning in the United States and around the world.

Europe faced not only economic depression but also, in the 1940s, another type of economic devastation, the physical destruction of cities and countryside by war. Both during and after World War II, many people were forced from their homes and countries of origin. Over 50 million people were killed by both the victorious Allied Powers, of which the United States was a member, and the Axis Powers. There was a need for reconstruction and renewal across Europe at this time.

As troops returned home, the United States experienced a period of growth, also known as a boom. Recognizing the need to assist veterans as they returned home from the front, on June 22, 1944, President Franklin D. Roosevelt signed the Servicemembers' Readjustment Act, also known as the GI Bill. Rather than providing welfare payments to veterans, something that was thought to diminish their incentive to reintegrate and work, the U.S. government decided to make post-secondary education—which up to that point was too expensive for most Americans to access—and home ownership possible. By the end of July 1956, 7.8 million veterans had received post-secondary education and 2.4 million veterans had received home loans guaranteed by the Department of Veterans Affairs.[25]

With an educated workforce, many veterans found employ-ment. The emergence of suburban communities, affordable single-family dwellings, and guaranteed loans opened the pos-sibility of home ownership to millions of families. Influencing urban planning (how a city's buildings, roads, and public spaces are organized) even today, the creation of roadways and the growth of the car culture provided an effective transporta-tion link between the suburbs and the cities.

Many couples were reunited after many months or even years apart. Between 1946 and 1964 a baby boom occurred, producing a generation known as the baby boomers, with over 76 million births in the United States during this period.[26] These new arrivals would continue to influence social trends and public policy from that period to the present.

CREATING THE IMF AND WORLD BANK IN THE POST-WORLD WAR II ECONOMY

Governments have an important role to play in managing the economic cycle, especially as it affects their countries. Although they cannot determine economic cycles affecting the entire world, governments are economic managers. They provide the guidance, expertise, and power to determine economic policies. Central banks, monetary policies, and balance of payments are examples of economic management. From time to time, however, governments do need financial assistance from outside sources. The World Bank and the IMF recognized this need, inspired, in part, by the work of British economist John Maynard Keynes.

In his most famous book, *The General Theory of Employment, Interest and Money*, Keynes suggested ways to improve the British economy during the 1930s. Keynes's ideas emerged from the needs of a country in crisis. The British economy faced many challenges during the Great Depression. Having been a leading force during World War I, Great Britain accumulated debts and saw a loss of the equivalent of $600 million dollars on its foreign investments. The disruption and loss of shipping trade routes saw a decline in customers for such goods as textiles, steel, and coal. Exports were at 80 percent, and industrial output ranged from 80 to 100 percent of the pre-World War I years. After the stock market crash of 1929, many countries implemented trade barriers (limits on the amount and type of trade permitted) and tariffs (taxes and fees). As demand for British products declined, exports fell in value by 50 percent, and unemployment increased from 1 million to 2.5 million in 1930. Drastic reductions in public spending and wages followed.[27]

Seeking to learn from and improve upon the British experience, Keynes came up with the idea of public work projects. Public works projects are publicly funded projects that improve the community; they include the building of roads, bridges, houses, schools, and libraries. They offer unemployed workers meaningful work and wages, which Keynes thought they would spend to support the economy. Keynes suggested the idea that governments must keep money in reserve in times of economic slowdown so they can employ people. The government, not private companies, must make these opportunities available to citizens.

Rather than relying upon private businesses to contribute, the founders of the World Bank and the IMF were inspired by the idea of guaranteed funds to support growth. With the financial and technical expertise provided by the World Bank and the IMF to governments, these funds and knowledge could be used to support the growth of publicly supported programs to assist with development and poverty reduction. The World Bank and the IMF received important political and financial support from U.S. President Franklin D. Roosevelt and U.S. Secretary of the Treasury Henry Morgenthau. Later, President Harry S. Truman also offered American support to these two new global organizations. Receiving this public support from the United States, which was increasing in global power and influence, helped

British economist John Maynard Keynes (*right*, meeting with U.S. Treasury Secretary Henry Morgenthau Jr.) was so influential that an entire modern school of economic thought was named after him: Keynesian economics. His theory that governments should invest in public works and hire the unemployed and his advocacy of spending during economic downturns was revolutionary. At the time, balanced budgets were common practice with the U.S. government, so his idea was met with opposition. Eventually, people were put back to work after the Great Depression, using public works projects.

make the World Bank a reality. The Articles of Agreement outline the purposes and goals of the World Bank:

i) To assist in the reconstruction and development of territories of members by facilitating the investment of capital for productive purposes, including the restoration of economies destroyed or disrupted by war, the reconversion of productive facilities to peacetime needs and the encouragement of the development of productive facilities and resources in less developed countries.

(ii) To promote private foreign investment by means of guarantees or participations in loans and other investments made by private investors; and when private capital is not available on reasonable terms, to supplement private investment by providing, on suitable conditions, finance for productive purposes out of its own capital, funds raised by it and its other resources.

(iii) To promote the long-range balanced growth of international trade and the maintenance of equilibrium in balances of payments by encouraging international investment for the development of the productive resources of members, thereby assisting in raising productivity, the standard of living and conditions of labor in their territories.

(iv) To arrange the loans made or guaranteed by it in relation to international loans through other channels so that the more useful and urgent projects, large and small alike, will be dealt with first.

(v) To conduct its operations with due regard to the effect of international investment on business conditions in the territories of members and, in the immediate postwar years, to assist in bringing about a smooth transition from a wartime to a peacetime economy.[28]

Seven hundred thirty delegates from 45 member countries signed the first Articles of the Agreement from July 1 to July 22, 1944. The World Bank made its first contribution, a loan of $250 million, to France in 1947 for the reconstruction of roads, transportation networks, ports, and buildings.[29]

The IMF, like the World Bank, was established at the United Nations International Monetary and Financial Conference in

Bretton Woods, New Hampshire. These Articles of Agreement of the IMF were approved by 29 countries. They came into effect on December 27, 1945.

i) To promote international monetary cooperation through a permanent institution which provides the machinery for consultation and collaboration on international monetary problems.

ii) To facilitate the expansion and balanced growth of international trade, and to contribute thereby to the promotion and maintenance of high levels of employment and real income and to the development of the productive resources of all members as primary objectives of economic policy.

iii) To promote exchange stability, to maintain orderly exchange arrangements among members, and to avoid competitive exchange depreciation.

iv) To assist in the establishment of a multilateral system of payments in respect of current transactions between members and in the elimination of foreign exchange restrictions which hamper the growth of world trade.

v) To give confidence to members by making the general resources of the Fund temporarily available to them under adequate safeguards, thus providing them with opportunity to correct maladjustments in their balance of payments without resorting to measures destructive of national or international prosperity.

vi) In accordance with the above, to shorten the duration and lessen the degree of disequilibrium in the international balances of payments of members.[30]

From March 8 to March 18, 1946, the Board of Governors of the IMF held its first meeting in Savannah, Georgia. In

(continues on page 52)

DEVASTATION IN FRANCE AT THE END OF WORLD WAR II AND THE START OF RECONSTRUCTION

The year is 1945. The sun breaks through the thick cloud cover as members of the 28th U.S. Infantry Division march proudly down the Champs-Élysées, the widest and most famous street in Paris. These soldiers, along with Allied Forces from countries like Canada and Great Britain, are received with smiles, cheers, and waves. The sounds of their marching feet, one after another after another, can be heard throughout the city. Happiness, pride, and even some fatigue can be heard in their footsteps. These steps are unlike the terrifying marches of the Nazis, the echoes of which were heard on this street mere hours ago. This city and this country have seen so much devastation in the last six years. Today, a day of celebration almost seems like a dream.

Some of the most famous parts of Paris, the Arc de Triomphe and the Eiffel Tower, are still standing. Tall green trees still line both sides of the Champs-Élysées. However, entire city blocks have been bombed, and the smell of smoldering ruins of some of these buildings hangs heavily in the air. Transportation networks, including railway lines and ports, have also been immobilized by the fighting and damage. Shards of glass and mangled pieces of steel abound. The broken glass and ruptured steel represent a country and a continent left as mere fragments of their former selves. Recognizing the need to rebuild, France's allies, especially the United States, are ready to help.

Two years later, in 1947, hope, not pain and horror, is on the mind of Robert Fortus. Fresh from a policy briefing at the American Embassy, Fortus, an international affairs advisor to the American ambassador, tries to move quickly. He is on a mission. With just five minutes to spare, he rushes up to the steps of the Élysée Palace, the official residence of the president of the French Republic. After checking in with the security desk, he is escorted to a dignified room with gold detailing on the ceiling. Paintings depicting France's illustrious history occupy each wall. Fortunately, the war has not encroached upon this elegant space.

Sitting down with his French counterpart, Monique Lavaure, he begins a diplomatic conversation about the Marshall Plan. Proud of her country's efforts during World War II but very mindful of the need for continued reconstruction, Lavaure says the French government is interested in participating in the Marshall Plan. Huge challenges confront this nation: industrial, urban, and agricultural planning are three areas of key concern. On a practical level, Fortus outlines how the Marshall Plan may forge a strong partnership between the United States and France to address these concerns. For instance, through the provision of loans to support industrial and urban planning, funds can be dedicated to rebuilding homes, businesses, and transportation hubs. This infrastructure may be used to facilitate trade between France and the United States. The sharing of best agricultural practices and subsidized grain products from the United States can assist with the renewal of the agricultural sector. As farmers begin to reclaim their land from trenches and destruction, these supports will enable them to farm once again. This diplomatic dialogue, one held quietly in a room in the Élysée Palace, is similar to other dialogues happening at this time across Europe. Such partnership efforts will continue throughout the 1940s as the World Bank and the IMF offer their support during this period of rebuilding and renewal.*

---

* Tony Judt. *Postwar: A History of Europe Since 1945.* (New York: Penguin, 2006).

(continued from page 49)
addition to adopting bylaws that governed the operations and electing the first executive director, the board agreed to locate the IMF headquarters in Washington, D.C. On May 6, 1946, the twelve executive directors held their first meeting in Washington, D.C., and the IMF began its operations on March 1, 1947. Again France was the first country to benefit, becoming the IMF's first client on May 8, 1945.

Reconstruction continued to be the main focus in the 1950s. In the 1960s, as Europe's former colonies won their independence, the World Bank focused on development. The changing institutional cultures of the 1970s, partly as a result of the opening of more country-based local field offices during this time, saw the World Bank seeking greater input and recognition at the country level. This was done to enable local citizens to offer their suggestions and input. Yet, critics of the World Bank and the IMF argue that their policies create modern forms of colonial dependence for developing countries. In the 1980s, the World Bank began to question its effectiveness. Specifically, one of its programs, structural adjustment, proved to be very controversial.

STRUCTURAL ADJUSTMENT PROGRAMS AND SENEGAL

Senegal, a West African country that was once a French colony, gained its independence from France in 1960. With independence came the big challenge of building a strong country. Although Senegal has a rich and long history, in modern terms, it was not a self-governing country until 1960. Senegal became one of the first countries to sign on for the structural adjustment program (SAP) in 1980. Senegal was experiencing economic declines, notably reduced exports and unemployment, in the early 1980s during a period of global recession (economic slowdown). The World Bank imposed many conditions on Senegal. It was required to focus its agricultural production on groundnuts, also known as peanuts. The World Bank hoped that this export would allow Senegal to earn enough money to repay its debt to the World Bank and to build the social supports its citizens needed. However, with most farmers growing groundnuts, Senegal had to import many other products for people to eat. This became expensive and added to Senegal's debt. In addition, there were massive droughts and crop failures. Other countries saw the potential benefits of exporting groundnuts. As a result, they decided to grow them too. With more competition, Senegalese farmers had to reduce prices so consumers would buy their groundnuts. When prices fell, the farmers earned less money. This economic downturn resulted in social unrest. In 2004, Senegal completed debt forgiveness and restructuring program offered by the World Bank and the IMF. Now, most groundnut production is privatized, largely through a company called Sonacos. Senegal continues to experience an annual growth rate of four percent a year.

Although there are many peanut farmers in the United States, the U.S. did not experience the same economic downturn. To make the crop competitive and appealing to farmers, the U.S. government provides subsidies, payments made by a government to a particular industry or part of the economy. Unfortunately for Senegal, the SAP agreement did not allow the government to subsidize its farmers.[31]

The World Bank learned from the experiences of Senegal. Since the 1990s, the World Bank has attempted to reconcile the impact of globalization (interconnection of people, communities, and nations around the world via trade, travel, media, and economic ties) with local needs while also promoting its programs. Good governance and the notion of development as freedom have emerged as key organizing themes during the current era.

Good governance means democratically elected and accountable government leaders. Responding to the criticism that the World Bank is still disconnected from the field, preferring Washington, D.C., as the site for negotiation and policy development, the World Bank established five "one country" trial programs in 2007. The United Nations, the World Bank, and the IMF, along with NGOs, government agencies, and other interested participants, are working together. These programs use a single country-based field office, a central budget provided to this office, and a locally deployed manager and her or his team. The one-country initiative is scheduled to expand to 20 programs in 2009, 40 programs in 2010, and to all other countries by 2012.[32] These changes, however, do not address all the concerns arising from the perceived distance of World Bank decision making from the realities of the field.

USING THE LESSONS OF HISTORY FOR THE POSSIBILITIES OF TODAY

The World Bank and the IMF were inspired by the big challenges of the Great Depression and World War II. Today, the goals of poverty reduction and development guide their work. Critics raise valid questions about the World Bank and the IMF, including concerns about the imposition of Western market practices and values upon non-Western economies, the enabling of dependence of developing countries on the World Bank and the IMF, debt repayment rather than the funding of programs, and the erosion of local, indigenous approaches to development in favor of those advocated by these institutions.

The economic and social losses of the period from 1929 to 1945 serve as powerful lessons about the need for globally applicable, coherent, and well-planned poverty reduction and development promotion strategies. The best practices of these eras continue to guide the policies of the World Bank and the IMF. The World Bank and the IMF provide useful examples of how loss, tragedy, and big social changes can influence programs resulting in global benefits.

How the
World Bank and
the IMF Help
Those in Need

IN 2007, THE WORLD BANK LOANED DEVELOPING COUNTRIES
nearly $25 billion dollars.[33] The World Bank offers long-term
loans to governments to financially support development
projects and economic reforms. These development projects
benefit the well-being of people in poor countries. They
include projects that extend health care, education, roads,
communications, and water treatment plants. Economic
changes make sure that the recipients' banking and other
financial systems, including the pensions, insurance, and central bank, are working well. If the economic system is strong,
then there will be more opportunities for the society and the
individuals in it to live fulfilling lives.

GETTING A LOAN FROM THE WORLD BANK

How does the World Bank decide who gets a loan? Major projects must be approved by vote of the World Bank Board, and the voting power of each country on the board is in proportion to the amount of contribution a country pays. The larger the economy, the more a country pays. As the country with the largest economy, the United States pays the largest fee. It also has the most voting power—16.4 percent of the total vote.

World Bank loans were originally given for specific projects. These projects included funds for roads, bridges, water purification plants, medical clinics, and schools. In the 1980s, the World Bank introduced the structural adjustment program (SAP). Allowing the recipient to have more discretion, these SAPs are more general loans for development.

One set of conditions attached to the loans relates to the way the country's economy is organized. Countries are required to open their economies to trade and investment. Various rules are removed to encourage other countries to trade and invest in these developing countries, such as opening access to markets by ending trade barriers (limits on products being exported and the quantities of exports), reducing tariffs (taxes and payments), and limiting subsidies (government payments to producers that reduce the costs of production); offering better exchange rates; and tax incentives (payments or other inducements). Investments may take the form of research building, building or expansion of companies, or direct foreign investment in local businesses.

Another condition of the loan is that the recipient country must transfer services that it has provided to private profit-making companies. As more services and programs are sold to private corporations, including things like utility companies selling water and electricity, the state has less control. This is known as privatization.

A country's currency can also be devalued, meaning it loses its value. Depending upon the terms of the arrangement

Many people fear that they will be unable to afford basic necessities like electricity, telephone service, and water if they are privatized and fall into the hands of private companies. Privatization is supported by the World Bank when administering loans to poor countries. *Above,* members of various nongovernmental organizations protest against the privatization of water resources in Bangalore, India, in 2004. The white disc at right shows an Indian coin with the three lions on the face being replaced by bottles of Coca Cola and Pepsi.

between the IMF and the country, countries can be compelled to devalue their currencies. When exchanged for other currencies, such as the euro, for instance, the U.S. dollar is worth less money.

Subsidies are not permitted. For example, to make European-produced agricultural products more appealing to buyers, the European Union provides subsidies in the form of cash payments to farmers. With this money, the farmers can charge lower prices. Since European consumers want to save money, they will be more likely to buy the European goods rather than the more expensive imported products. Richer countries continue to provide subsidies to their farmers who need them, but developing countries must meet rigid demands without the benefit of subsidies.

As part of the SAPs, countries are expected to increase their exports, especially exports of cash crops (agricultural products with high consumer demand and profitability outside the country in which they are produced) and natural resources. As exports grow, so does the amount of money coming in to a country. Ideally, but not always in reality, this money can be used to help repay the loan from the World Bank or the IMF, reduce poverty, and encourage development. Increased exports also help to keep the currency stable.

Countries that want assistance must approach the International Bank for Reconstruction and Development (IBRD) and the International Development Association (IDA). The IBRD has money that comes from the financial contributions made by member countries. It also raises money by selling AAA-rated bonds, the highest rating available. The AAA rating assures investors that the money they invest will be safe and returned with interest. A bond is a type of debt. An investor loans money to an organization or company in return for a rate of interest. For example, an investor, usually a government or big corporation, buys a bond from the IBRD for $1 million. After a year, that investor will get its money back in addition to the interest it has accrued or generated. If the bond's interest rate is 2 percent, for instance, the investor will get the original sum back (the $1 million) plus the interest amount of $20,000.

The IBRD also funds the day-to-day operations of the World Bank. These are known as the operating expenses. These expenses include the salaries of the World Bank's employees, security, construction and maintenance of buildings, heat, electricity, water, and insurance. The IBRD also contributes funds to debt relief and the IDA. The IDA provides the greatest number of interest-free loans of any of organization in the world. It is a big challenge to find the money necessary to fund these loans. There are two issues. First, these are loans that do not gain interest or funds from the recipients. Second, the amount of money being loaned is huge. Where does the money come from? Fortunately, the 40 member countries with the largest economies contribute the funds needed to keep the IDA working and loaning money. The funds are replaced every three years. As the largest economy in the world, the United States plays a key role in supporting the IDA fund. Additional funds are provided by the repayment of loans after a 35- to 40-year term.

The IBRD and IDA provide two types of loans: investment loans and development policy loans. Investment loans are provided to support economic and social development projects. Development policy loans support a country's policy and institutional reforms. Examples of policy and institutional reforms include reorienting a country's economic system to open and accessible trade and capital investment; supporting democratic development through the sharing of expertise and best practices in such areas as electoral and judicial reform and the training of government employees; and the promotion of democratic development through public information campaigns via television, radio, the Internet, and community forums.

If a country wants funds, it must submit a formal letter that outlines its project. The project must be economically, financially, socially, and environmentally acceptable to the World Bank. Then, a country submits a formal application. This application includes written reports, ongoing meetings and interviews of governmental officials by World Bank representatives, site visits to the country, and discussions with communities and nongovernmental organizations. A country must show that it will meet the development objectives of poverty reduction and increased development. It must describe specifically what will result from the financial assistance. It must include goals for improvement in things like the life expectancy rate (how long someone in that country, on average, lives), the infant mortality rate (the number of deaths of children aged one year or less per 1,000 births), and the literacy rate (the number of people who can read and write). The country outlines a month-by-month and year-by-year timeline of what it will do to reduce poverty and increase development.

Finally, a schedule is created by the World Bank indicating when and how the money will be provided to the country. The money is transferred directly by the World Bank and the IMF to the national treasury (the central government-run bank) of a country. The IDA also provides grants to address issues and support civil society groups. For example, grant money has been used to improve sanitation, increased HIV/AIDS awareness and prevention efforts, ease the debt burden, and support civil society organizations.

SAPS: MORE HARM THAN GOOD?

SAPs remain one of the most controversial aspects of the World Bank and the IMF operations. Repayment is a continuing issue with these loans since they are conditional. Money is provided with the expectation and agreement that it will be repaid. Even with relatively low interest rates, countries have had to rearrange their entire economies to repay the loans. Many countries found themselves in the unfortunate position of having to repay—or service—their debts or interest on the debts instead of developing social and development programs for their citizens.

SAPs were popular during the 1980s. Today, critics argue that requiring developing countries to reduce spending on social programs and benefits, including education and health care, in favor of repaying debts to the World Bank and the IMF, puts the needs of the World Bank and the IMF ahead of the citizens, especially the poorest citizens, of these developing countries. The standard of living had to be lowered to meet the terms of the loans. For example, no country in Africa has been able to meet the terms of debt rescheduling since 1983.

This debt amounted to $218 billion in 1987. That huge figure represents three times Africa's export earnings.[34]

When faced with a debt repayment dilemma, developing countries are sometimes forced to make sacrifices. What workers are paid and safety on the job usually decreases, in such circumstances. As governments spend more money to repay the debt, they spend less money on social programs. This can lead to social unrest. For example, since less money may be spent on health care, then there will be increased infant and child mortality. If water services are privatized, as they were in Bolivia in support of that country's SAP, then people may not be able to afford enough clean water to live. These results are contrary to the goals of the World Bank and the IMF.

Another example, but with a more positive conclusion, can be found in Ecuador. With a year-round climate ideal for rose production, along with the money directed to economic growth in the form of an extensive network of greenhouses and production facilities, Ecuador is now one of the world's leading exporters of roses to the United States, Canada, and Western Europe. Recognized by the World Bank and the IMF as a cash crop, roses have generated sufficient income for agricultural development, crop diversification, and environmental sustainability.

Responding to the criticisms of SAPs, the International Financial Institution Advisory Commission released the Meltzer Report in 2000. Headed by Professor Allan Meltzer of Carnegie Mellon University, the report supported debt forgiveness, not SAPs, for the poorest countries. Today, the World Bank and the IMF are embracing debt forgiveness for the most heavily indebted countries. Known as the HIPC Program (Heavily Indebted Poor Countries Initiative), the World Bank and the IMF are canceling two-thirds of the debt of the poorest and most indebted countries. In return, these countries must work with the World Bank and the IMF to reorganize their national budgets and spending so they will invest in social improvements like education and health care. In July 2005,

Since 1991, the United States has had a pact with Peru, Colombia, Bolivia, and Ecuador to allow them to send goods duty free in exchange for a crackdown on the production of cocaine and other drugs. This has been a great deal for Ecuador in particular, because its flourishing rose business has contributed $300 million to its economy. Women predominantly do the picking, pruning, and packaging. Although concerns have arisen about low wages and the effects of long-term exposure to pesticides, workers insist that these jobs are essential because they provide financial independence.

leaders of the world's richest countries agreed to cancel the debts held by the 18 poorest countries.

The World Bank has gone even further in helping poor countries tackle poverty. By moving away from SAPs to the Poverty Reduction Strategy Paper, the World Bank has shown it is more interested in seeing the interconnections between social growth and development policy. Intended to promote social growth and reduce poverty, this approach goes beyond

BRINGING THE INTERNET TO THE PEOPLE

Drishtee is a company that links rural Indian villages to the Internet. It won a grant of $68,500 from the World Bank's Development Marketplace competition. First offered in 1998, the Development Marketplace provides funds to grassroots, also known as community-based, leaders and organizations that are fighting poverty through a variety of means. Youth, universities, businesses, and other community groups may apply. The award promotes innovation and problem solving with various partners within the government, industry, banks, and communities. Since its creation, more than 1,000 projects in more than 70 countries have received Development Marketplace awards totaling over $40 million.

This global competition for funds is held every 12 to 18 months. Other recent winners of the competition include recycling projects in Burkina Faso and the planting of chili peppers in Zimbabwe to protect crops from elephants.[*]

Just as when a country applies for funding, Drishtee had to submit a formal application, although a much shorter one. By providing Internet kiosks equipped with computers, printers, generators, digital cameras, and wireless connections, Drishtee is connecting rural India with the world. Today, there are 1,700 Drishtee entrepreneurs operating in 12 states throughout India. They serve 15 million rural residents. In 2008, Drishtee will expand to 10,000 kiosks across India. Local artists and small business owners, once dependent upon buyers to negotiate prices for their goods, can now use the Internet to work directly with retailers. In turn, they are able to set more competitive—and profitable—prices.

---

[*] World Bank. "Development Marketplace: Competitions." Available online at *http://web.worldbank.org/WBSITE/EXTERNAL/OPPORTUNITIES/GRANTS/DEVMARKETPLACE/0,,contentMDK:21617862~pagePK:180691~piPK:174492~theSitePK:205098,00.html.*

economic changes and debt repayment to larger social reforms. Although the World Bank must see how the money is being used, countries have greater control.

Besides providing funds, the World Bank provides advice. The World Bank is committed to capacity building within its client countries. As countries acquire the skills, policies, and institutions for poverty reduction and development promotion, they can make positive changes. This is called capacity building. For instance, capacity building includes the promotion of gender equality to facilitate participation by women and girls. By seeking input from communities about addressing gender biases, a cross section of women and girls have the opportunity to share their insights during program planning and implementation. Capacity building also entails the provision of technical expertise to develop and strengthen educational systems, transportation networks, alternative fuel sources, and health care.

To support country-based capacity building, the World Bank is helping its employees learn more about poverty reduction and development. By doing so, the World Bank hopes to build the capacity—the current ability and future potential—in its policies and programs to do a better job. World Bank employees are expected to participate in ongoing learning. The World Bank provides many opportunities for learning. For instance, the Global Development Learning Network is a type of online distance education available to employees and World Bank partners. The World Bank Institute offers Global and Regional Programs and B-Span (Internet-based broadcasting) to promote ongoing learning and best practices.

THE IMF IN ACTION

The IMF works to promote the well-being of the financial system. Its does so via surveillance, its lending programs, and the provision of technical assistance. Technical assistance takes many forms: foreign exchange and capital market development, deposit insurance (providing security for investors by

Historically, the IMF's managing director has been European and the World Bank's president has been American. Recently, this standard has been questioned by critics who claim that the executive board rarely votes against American or European interests. Competition for these two posts may soon open to include candidates from other parts of the world. Pictured are IMF Managing Director Dominique Strauss-Kahn *(right)* and World Bank President Robert Zoellick *(left)* in April 2008.

guaranteeing that their deposited money will be protected by the government), and legal supports and regulations for banking (i.e., fraud prevention). In addition, the Financial Sector Assessment Program, launched in 1999, is a joint World Bank-IMF program to evaluate the well being of financial systems.

In keeping with tradition, the managing director of the IMF is from Europe. The current managing director is Dominique Strauss-Kahn from France. His job is to oversee all IMF operations. At the top of the IMF's organizational structure is the

Board of Governors. There is one governor from each of the 185 member countries. Each member country appoints one governor and one alternate governor. Together, they serve a five-year term, but may be reappointed by the member country. Ministers of finance or ministers of development are usually appointed to these positions. The governors meet once per year at the joint IMF–World Bank meetings. The 24 governors, representing the most powerful country members, including the United States, sit on the International Monetary and Finance Committee and meet twice a year. The governors' duties include admitting or suspending membership privileges to countries, determining how money will be spent, and reviewing financial reports.

Daily operations at the headquarters in Washington, D.C., are overseen by the 24-member executive board. In keeping with tradition and because the United States is the largest shareholder, the president of the World Bank is American. Robert B. Zoellick is the current president. Europe and America's influence over the selection of the president of the World Bank and the managing director of the IMF has been criticized. Leaders from developing countries, along with their personal experiences with and responses to poverty and underdevelopment, are denied access to these pivotal roles.

GETTING A LOAN FROM THE IMF

Similar to the process for getting a loan from the World Bank, countries seeking support from the IMF send an official letter of intent to the executive board. This letter, written by the minister of finance, outlines all of the financial policies a country will undertake in support of its request for financial support. Member countries may borrow at a low interest rate through the Poverty Reduction and Growth Facility and the Exogenous Shocks Facility. Loans with low interest rates include the Stand-by Arrangement, the Supplemental Reserve Facility, and the Compensatory Financing Facility.

- The Stand-by Arrangements are held by countries to address short-term balance of payment problems. Loan repayments are usually made between 2.3 years and 4 years. The Extended Fund Facility, created in 1974, helps countries to address longer-term balance of payment problems. Repayment occurs between 4.5 years and 7 years.

- The Supplemental Reserve Facility, introduced in 1997, provides short-term financing (or funds) on a large scale. This program was originally created to provide money to support the growth of export markets and investments within developing markets. Foreign investment is needed to help build these markets. However, if foreign investors lose confidence in a country, then capital flight can happen. Capital flight occurs when investors remove their investments— money, expertise, employment opportunities, trade, and materials—from an economy. Capital flight is bad for a country because it means the loss of partnerships, investment, and opportunities for growth. The more foreign investment there is in a country, the more appealing the country looks to other countries for investment and trade. These loans are usually repaid within 2 to 2.5 years, but there is a 3 to 5 percent surcharge that must be paid by the member country.

- The Compensatory Financing Facility, established in 1963, provides funds to developing countries that experience a loss in export earnings or to help pay for more expensive cereal imports. A loss in export earnings means that the cost of exports, due to reduced demand, for example, decreases. When this happens, a country does not make as much money from the goods it sells or exports to other countries. Cereal imports, including whole grains like wheat, millet, barley, rice, and oats, are important parts of many diets and for farming. For example, these grains, or their by-products, may be fed to humans and livestock. When the cost of these items increases because of crop failures, for example, then countries may need assistance in purchasing these goods. Although there is no surcharge on this loan, repayment occurs between 2.3 and 4 years.

Emergency funds are also provided to member countries after natural disasters. Since 1962, the IMF has provided over $2.9 billion to 38 countries in the form of emergency assistance.[35] These loans must be repaid between 3.3 and 5 years. Member countries requesting this emergency assistance must show how the funds will be used in support of the IMF's performance criteria. A country may be granted between 25 to 50 percent of its quota, the amount the member country contributes to the IMF, in emergency assistance. The greater the destruction, the more likely it is that a country will receive a larger amount of money. It is like a form of financial insurance. For example, the Indian government accessed this money to set up temporary shelters and field hospitals immediately after the Asian Tsunami in 2004. Today, there are warning signs about tsunamis on Indian beaches.

THE WORLD BANK AND THE IMF PROGRAMS

Since 1989, to avoid overlap and duplication, the World Bank and the IMF have been working closely together. The two organizations share information and expertise in a variety of ways: joint country missions (the World Bank and the IMF share information and resources when visiting and working with a country); sharing of development progress by World Bank experts with financial assessments by the IMF experts; the president of the World Bank and the managing director of the IMF meet regularly; annual joint meetings of the boards of governors of the World Bank and the IMF provide opportunities for joint planning; semiannual meetings of the development committee provides opportunities for sharing ideas and problem solving; directors who sit on the executive boards of the World Bank and the IMF meet three times per week at the Washington, D.C., headquarters.

The two organizations also have launched key policies together. The first one, created in 1996, is the Heavily Indebted Poor Countries (HIPC) Initiative. In 1999, the World Bank and the IMF created the Poverty Reduction Strategy Paper (PRSP). The World Bank and the IMF work with countries to link development policies, government spending, and financial and technical support from the World Bank and the IMF to reduce poverty. In 1999, the IMF introduced the Poverty Reduction and Growth Facility (PRGF) program. Being country-owned, with input from the communities and governments directly affected, the PRFG program seeks increased public participation, countries having greater say and responsibility for development, and a commitment to good governance. This means that government leaders are elected in democratic, fair, and accountable ways. As of August 2007, 78 low-income countries were eligible for PRGF support.[36] Responding to criticisms that the Millennium Development Goals to reduce poverty by half by the year 2015 were unrealistic, in 2004 the World Bank and the IMF introduced the Global Monitoring Report (GMR). This report provides annual updates about how well the Millennium Development Goals are being met.

In 2005, the HIPC Initiative was supplemented by the Multilateral Debt Relief Initiative (MDRI). This allows for 100 percent of relief on eligible debts by the IMF, IDA, the African Development Fund, and the Inter-American Development Bank. The African Development Fund and the Inter-American Development Bank, as the names suggest, are support organizations geared to the specific needs of the two regions: Africa and North, Central, and South America. (The Asian Development Bank supports that region.)

Following extensive lobbying by nongovernmental organizations and other bodies, the World Bank and the IMF created in 1996 the Heavily Indebted Poor Countries program to provide debt relief and low-interest loans to countries they have identified as needing special assistance to reduce external debt repayments. In 2004, with its debts totaling $6.5 billion and more than half of its population living in poverty, Nicaragua qualified for major debt concessions equaling more than $4 billion. Here, a girl walks into her kitchen in Managua, Nicaragua.

But even if all of the debts were forgiven by the MDRI, this does not solve all of the problems. To be considered, a country must meet some requirements. First, the country must have an unsustainable debt burden. This means that if the debt and payment of interest were to continue, then the country might go bankrupt or be unable to provide the basics of life to its citizens. Second, the country must be eligible for IDA and PRGF funding. Third, the country must show a track record of effective reforms. These reforms could include efforts to build schools and increase the number of girls receiving an education, the development of effective and reliable banking systems, or the creation of water purification plants. Fourth, the country must create a poverty reduction strategy paper (PRSP). Similar to a research report, the country outlines in detail the work it has done and will do to reduce poverty and promote development.

Upon approval, a country then must pass through a series of support stages: it reduces debt to the sustainability threshold (meaning the country has less debt that it can maintain or service via interest payments); it receives interim relief from the World Bank and the IMF; and, once the country has shown positive reforms, the country reaches the completion point. To date, 41 countries are eligible for debt forgiveness by the MDRI. This will cost $68 billion. The IMF is paying this big price tag from the proceeds of gold sales. Member countries pay their membership fees via cash and, if they choose, gold payment. The gold payment comes in the form of gold bullion or bars. Twenty-two countries have reached the completion point.[37] Ten countries are at the decision point, the point when the World Bank decides whether to go ahead with the support.

During the annual meeting September 24 and 25, 2005, the governors of the World Bank and the IMF supported the G-8 countries' proposal to cancel the multilateral debts of the 18 poorest countries. The G-8 countries, the eight richest countries in the world, include the United States, Canada, Italy, France, Germany, the United Kingdom, Japan, and Russia. The support of the G-8 also comes from greater public awareness about debt and debt forgiveness. Even pop music stars, including Bono of U2, have promoted debt forgiveness in his music and activism.

FROM ASSISTANCE TO AUTONOMY

As large global organizations, the daily operations of the World Bank and the IMF are complex, bureaucratic, and not necessarily accessible to the average person, whether one is located in Togo, Indonesia, or the United States. As transparency, accountability, responsiveness, and equality come to inform all aspects of the programs emerging from the World Bank and the IMF, there are more opportunities for people to share their voices and experiences as part of program development and implementation. The World Bank and the IMF also seek out both the large- and small-scale opportunities for this type of civic involvement. This is the human face of poverty reduction and development promotion.

The World Bank and the International Monetary Fund in Africa and Asia

WITH THEIR GLOBAL SCOPE, WIDE-RANGING POLICIES AND programs, and ambitious goals, the size and influence of the World Bank and the IMF can overshadow the particularities of the clients—the people and communities—they serve. This discussion considers the work of these organizations in the contexts of continental Africa and Asia.

Africa is the largest continental client served by the World Bank and the IMF. As the world's second largest continent, Africa is home to 53 countries and more than 922 million people. Asia, the second largest continental client served by the World Bank and the IMF, is the fourth largest and most populace continent. Asia is home to more than 4 billion people—60 percent of the world's population—and 37 countries. Each continent, with its particular development needs and demographics (segments of the population), presents unique challenges and opportunities for the World Bank and the IMF.

GLOBALIZING AFRICA: RECONSIDERING EAST VERSUS WEST

When one considers the complex and varied colonial history of Africa, a long lineage of Western influence is evident. From the first Greek mercantile colony established at Naucratis (modern-day Egypt) to the redrawing of national boundaries during the "Scramble for Africa" during the late eighteenth century—an act of forced nationhood by such colonial proponents as Cecil Rhodes, Lord Frederick Lugard, and countless European missionaries—Africa has been the subject of colonial control. At that time, the prevailing view equated colonization with salvation. African colonization was motivated by greed, power, and racism. This racist viewpoint would guide the colonial period.

Upon decolonization, largely during the post-World War II era, and in response to growing nationalism, African countries began to redefine such key issues as poverty and development within their own contexts. In response, the World Bank Group's Africa Action Plan, a three-year initiative, which included the support of the IMF, focused on development and poverty reduction in the following key areas: strengthening the private sector; increasing economic empowerment of women; building skills for competitiveness in the global economy; raising agricultural productivity; improving access to and reliability of clean energy; expanding and upgrading road networks and transit corridors; increasing access to safe water and sanitation; and strengthening national health systems to combat malaria and HIV/AIDS.[38] Recent indicators demonstrate progress; economic growth in Africa averaged 5.5 percent in 2005 and 5.3 percent in 2006, respectively; primary school enrollment increased to 96 percent in 2004; and the child mortality rate fell from 161 per 1,000 births in 1990 to 149 per 1,000 births in 2004.[39]

The World Bank and the IMF have financed various projects in Madagascar, Africa, such as improving transport and infrastructure and supporting health programs. Organizations such as Mad'Eole are also involved in the fight against poverty by financing a wind farm that will bring electricity and jobs to 15 villages. Pictured is a woman walking past three eco-friendly windmills in the Sahasifotra village in Madagascar.

THE DOHA DEVELOPMENT AGENDA

Compelling in its appeal to intercultural dialogue, discourse on globalization has implications for standards of living and development for billions of people worldwide. Considering globalization in action, the 2001 Doha Round (*round* means "negotiations") conducted by the World Trade Organization (WTO) are instructive. The WTO is an international organization dealing with the rules of trade between countries. It helps to mediate disputes arising from trade issues, including tariffs, over- and underproduction of goods, and subsidies. The Doha Round, the inspiration for the Doha Development Agenda advocated by the World Bank and the IMF, proposed increased market access for developing countries as a means to achieve economic growth and poverty reduction. On November 14, 2001, the Doha Round produced a ministerial declaration. A ministerial declaration is when all of the government ministers, or key politicians, agree on a plan of action and present it in writing. In it, developing countries were explicitly acknowledged as trade partners. In it, developing countries were explicitly acknowledged as trade partners.[40]

The ministerial declaration recognizes the importance of international trade as a place for competitiveness and development for less-developed countries (LDCs). However, developed countries often benefit from unfair market advantage, such as subsidies, and self-determined market conditions, such as domestic support. Despite claims of equal access, it is acknowledged that LDCs hold a unique place: "We agree that special and differential treatment for developing countries shall be an integral part of all elements of the negotiations and shall be embodied in the schedules of concessions . . . and as appropriate in the rules and disciplines to be negotiated."[41]

Burkina Faso, a country in West Africa, provides an instructive example of Africa's efforts to negotiate its needs, especially its global competitiveness, within today's postcolonial and globally competitive era. Burkina Faso relies upon cotton as a significant export, accounting for approximately 6.5 percent of its GDP, 66 percent of agriculture earnings, and 33 percent of overall export revenues.[42] These figures need to be considered within the wider marketplace as cotton production increased and export earnings fell by one-third between 1999 and 2002. By contrast, the International Cotton Advisory Committee (ICAC) reported cotton subsidies amount to $5.8 billion. The largest beneficiaries of subsidies were the United States ($3.3 billion) and the European Union ($1.1 billion).[43] In 2001, the cost of a cotton bushel was $0.9313, and the export price was $0.3968 a bushel.[44] The subsidy amounted to $0.55. From 1995 to 2001, American dumping (flooding the market with excess subsidized products) of cotton increased from 17 percent to 57 percent.[45] In response, during the April 2003 WTO round, Burkina Faso, in conjunction with the African nations of Benin, Chad, and Mali, submitted a cotton proposal seeking the end of preferential subsidies and dumping by developed countries; however, the proposal was not well received.

Rather than addressing the economic advantage of subsidized cotton from the United States or the European Union, the proposed economic diversification, especially in the wake of structural readjustment, is neither possible nor desirable. Opponents of the ministerial declaration have gone further, advocating the removal of agriculture entirely from the WTO, ending cotton subsidies in developed countries, and promoting the growth and sale of organic cotton. A letter of intent from Jean-Baptiste Compaoré, minister of finance and budget minister for the government of Burkina Faso, to the IMF, dated December 20, 2004, outlines the domestic and international challenges facing the country:

> The government of Burkina Faso is implementing a program of macroeconomic and structural reforms for the period 2003–2006 with the support of the

International Monetary Fund (the IMF). A three-year arrangement under the Poverty Reduction and Growth Facility (PRGF), for an amount equivalent to SDR 24.08 million (40 percent of quota), was approved by the IMF Board on June 11, 2003. We are making satisfactory progress under this arrangement, despite a recent substantial deterioration of Burkina Faso's external environment. Specifically, the economy is coping with record low cotton prices, a sharp increase in oil prices, a drought in the north of the country, the locust infestation in the Sahel, the situation in Côte d'Ivoire, and the recent strong appreciation of the euro.[46]

Access to fair global market share is important for increased poverty reduction and development promotion. It is no longer sufficient to assume the cotton growers of Burkina Faso are distant and disconnected from our lives; globalization compels one to question and lobby for fairer trade agreements, as well as improved and sustainable standards of living. This transparency offers promise. Supported by the World Bank and the IMF, the Doha Development Agenda (DDA) provides a framework for more equitable trade practices. This more responsive globalization reflects—or has the potential to reflect—the needs of LDCs. While neither trade nor globalization is entirely neutral or even benevolent, there is the possibility for assertion of local needs within a global forum.

Developing countries need to approach globalization in a different way than the developed countries. Alliance building within and across continents offers one possibility. Although the experiences of poverty and underdevelopment vary widely from one country to another, there is a common need to forge strategic partnerships, as demonstrated by the alliance between cotton-producers Burkina Faso, Benin, Chad, and Mali. These alliances are made possible and rendered effective within a globalized sphere. The globalized system works to limit and promote trade as well as development in this context; however, the lessons of Doha necessitate greater public scrutiny of how trade policy is implemented. It must be seen to be implemented fairly to ensure equitable access to market share and, in so doing, access to development.

There is a need for a wider understanding of how globalization interconnects culture, economics, security, and development. The example of cotton growers in Burkina Faso is helpful in seeing the need to reclaim globalization as a forum that supports local diversity, including the economic imperative of ensuring a fair and sustainable market price for Burkina Faso's cotton exports, while remaining globally competitive. As stated in a report at the UN's 2003 Globalization with a Human Face conference, "We must shift our emphasis and purpose to ecological globalization, to social globalization, to the globalization of employment, and to the globalization of rights."[47] Similarly, the "globalization of values," developed during the Economic Commission for Latin America and the Caribbean (ECLAC) summit, advocates "the gradual spread of shared ethical principles whose clearest manifestations are the declarations on the two main dimensions of human rights—civil and political rights, and economic, social, and cultural rights—and the declarations issued at world summits held by the UN, including, most notably, the millennium declaration."[48] Globalization need not be a homogenizing process, disempowering, or reinforcing a contemporary version of the East versus West divide. Informed by a human rights imperative, including the right to earn a living, fair trade and labor practices, and environmental sustainability, this approach has the potential to achieve an adequate supply of global public goods, gradually overcoming global inequities, and establishing a rights-based international social agenda.

The issues of fair wages for the cotton grower, a marketable price for the cotton bushel, and Burkina Faso's economic needs may be raised using this international forum, the global media, and working with NGOs to advocate humane and person-focused trade practices. When people reconsider the dichotomy of the protestor versus the trade negotiator, what emerges is an engaged, participatory vision of globalization that transcends this divide to include the cotton farmer, harvester, government minister, trade representative, protestor, and consumer within the globalized web of interrelations and mutual responsibilities.

THE WORLD BANK AND EDUCATION IN AFRICA: A CASE STUDY OF THE AFRICAN VIRTUAL UNIVERSITY

Responding to the need for accessible education and the reality that more than half of Africa's 700 million people are under the age of 20, the World Bank helped to set up the African Virtual University (AVU). Now an independent intergovernmental organization based in Nairobi, Kenya, the AVU has 34 learning centers in 17 African countries. An intergovernmental organization works with governments to achieve access. In this case, the AVU coordinates the delivery of educational programming by working with 17 African governments. No single government owns the program. Instead, the governments work together to make educational access possible for students across the African continent. The World Bank is the largest supporter of the AVU, having committed over $13 million over three years.

The AVU has also launched an accredited degree and diploma in computer science. More than 23,000 students are registered in its courses. An additional 2,500 professionals are enrolled in its business seminars. Current course offerings include Web site development and maintenance, English for academics and business, the history of renewable energy sources, and how to harness solar power.

THE WORLD BANK AND
HIV AND AIDS AWARENESS:
THE MULTI-COUNTRY AIDS PROGRAM

HIV and AIDS are two of the most critical public health issues in the world today. No matter where you live, no matter your gender, age, sexual orientation, class position, or culture, you can be infected by HIV and AIDS. Continental Africa has the highest rate of HIV and AIDS cases in the world. Funsani, a 15-year-old boy from Malawi, walks over to the local health clinic (funded and built, in part, by the support of the World Bank and the IMF) near his home in Lilongwe, the capital city. The estimated HIV prevalence rate in Malawi is 14.1 percent among 14- to 49-year-olds.[49]

Along the way, Funsani notices that a couple of the HIV and AIDS awareness posters have been defaced. After he asks the clinic manager about the graffiti, she offers to replace the posters. Mindful of the stigma and silence surrounding HIV and AIDS and recalling the ostracism of a former classmate who become infected with the AIDS virus, Funsani asks the manager how else this prevention message can be shared with young people. Thanks to his own Internet research and global awareness, Funsani offers some great suggestions for spreading the message of prevention, such as interactive role-plays, graphic novels, and Internet sites for young people. Of course, whether these suggestions can be realized is another question. Is there enough money? Will the community be supportive? Will this prevention campaign make a positive difference? Is the technology available to make Internet access and web development possible and effective? The inability to access computer technology due to insufficient funds is known as the digital divide. Fortunately, since HIV and AIDS are priority areas for the World Bank, additional funds are available for this type of work. Funsani's activism shows the power of what is possible in one's own community. One person can make a difference.

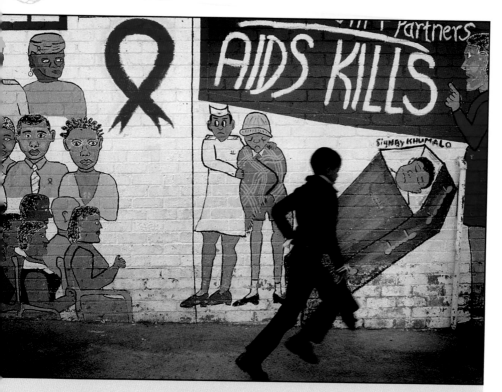

According to the World Bank, in Africa alone, 13 million children have lost one or both parents to AIDS. The virus continues to spread, with new epidemics erupting in China, Indonesia, Papua New Guinea, Vietnam, several central Asian republics, and the Baltic states. In the last five years, the Multi-country HIV/AIDS Program (MAP) for Africa has contributed $1.5 billion to 33 countries. Total financing from the World Bank for HIV/AIDS since 1988 is approximately $4 billion.

Responding to the HIV and AIDS epidemics throughout Africa, the World Bank created the Multi-Country AIDS Program (MAP). Launched in 2000, it originally committed $1 billion to fight HIV/AIDS in sub-Saharan Africa (the region lying south of the Sahara Desert). Since then, funding has increased to $10 billion. Between 40 and 60 percent of this money, depending on the country, is directed to civil society—or nongovernmental—

organizations.[50] MAP has created National AIDS authorities within the offices of the president or prime minister in each of the 28 participating countries.

The need is great. Sub-Saharan Africa represents 0.7 billion of the total global population—or 700 million—people. This region is extremely poor. The average annual income is $490, and 47 countries in the region are eligible for World Bank and IMF funding. (To date, the World Bank has loaned $4.1 billion to the region.) The average life expectancy in the region is 46 years. Twenty-three percent of girls cannot read or write. An estimated 25.2 million people are living with HIV and AIDS in the region.[51] This is astounding considering worldwide there are approximately 33 million people living with HIV and AIDS. However, the number of cases in sub-Saharan Africa is probably much bigger because many people, fearful of social stigma, will not get tested. MAP is working to end the stigma.

ASIAN DEVELOPMENT IN ACTION

Like Africa, Asia has a history of colonialism. Asia traces its colonial roots to the first European voyages to seek a passage to India during the late fifteenth century, which created spice routes between Asia and Europe. This was followed by Portuguese control of key waterways between the Indian Ocean and Europe during the sixteenth century, and the final large-scale colonial scramble—often referred to as the New Imperialism—saw European powers, including Great Britain, France, and Belgium, clamoring for access to such primary resources as silk, cotton, tea, and spices. As in Africa, throughout Asia, the post-World War II period, along with increasing nationalism, helped disrupt colonial ties in favor of national sovereignty.

Modern-day efforts by the World Bank and the IMF to address poverty and underdevelopment tend to be coun-try-specific and community-specific, rather than continental approaches, such as the Africa Action Plan.

The Grameen Bank and Microcredit—
An Asian Success Story with Global Benefits

While Africa is considered a leader in such areas as online learning and HIV and AIDS awareness and prevention strategies, Asia is also a development leader. Microcredit, also known as microfinance, is one example of local Asian innovation with global benefits.

The term *microcredit* is fairly new. It only came into popular usage in the 1970s. Microcredit refers to credit on a small scale. Small loans are given to people to start or sustain a business. The idea was first proposed by Dr. Muhammad Yunus, a Bangladeshi economist. Microfinance provides credit to people lacking financial resources. Traditional banks are typically not interested in loaning money to people with low socioeconomic status for two reasons. First, the amount of money they want to borrow tends to be very small. As a result, the amount of interest (profit) a bank will gain is also small. Second, these borrowers have little money or property to serve as collateral for their loans. Collateral refers to the things of value a person owns, including stocks, bonds, and real estate or property, that they can offer the lender in case they are unable to repay the loan. If they are unable to repay the loan, then the lender can claim ownership of the collateral. Many poor people do not have collateral. If they default on the loan—meaning they cannot pay the loan back—then the bank has lost the money it has loaned to the person or business.

Seeing credit as a human right, microfinance provides poor people with access to savings, credit, insurance, and other financial services. With credit comes the ability to build businesses, become financially strong, and, by doing so, to be a fully active and empowered individual. By helping poor people, especially women, overcome poverty, all of society benefits. Microcredit brings the bank to the people, not the other way around.

Grameen, a Bangla word taken from the language spoken in Bangladesh, means "the Bank of the Villages." Since becom-

Thanks to the Grameen Bank, this Bangladeshi carpenter has a successful shop in Manikganj, Bangladesh. The bank makes small loans, known as microcredit, to poor people without requiring collateral. Started in 1976, there are now 2,100 branches, and its success has inspired similar projects in more than 40 countries. The World Bank has also financed Grameen-type ventures throughout the world, and Grameen Bank's founder Dr. Muhammad Yunus received the Nobel Peace Prize in 2006.

ing an independent bank in October 1983, as decreed by the Bangladeshi government, the Grameen Bank derives its capital (money) from three primary sources: donor agencies (including the World Bank), the Bangladeshi government, and bond sales. The Bangladeshi government and bond sales are the main capital sources today.[52]

Loans are provided through community-based non-profit organizations. Recipients pay the loans back in weekly, monthly, or yearly installments. In fact, the loan repayment rate is much higher in a microcredit arrangement than with traditional banks. Why? Trust plays a big role. Since recipients are getting loans from community organizations, not large and impersonal banks, there is a desire to keep the personal bonds of trust, mutual respect, and integrity strong. One powerful way to do this is to repay the loan. Recipients usually reserve the profits from their business for growth of the business.

Dr. Muhammad Yunus, the founder of the Grameen Bank, received the Nobel Peace Prize in 2006. The World Bank supports microcredit by providing funding and technical support. The World Bank and the IMF see microcredit as a tool for development and as an opportunity for people to decide how to invest in their own communities for positive change. The World Bank also cites microcredit as one important source of women's empowerment.[53] After endorsing the International Year of Microcredit in 2005, the World Bank increased its involvement by exercising its ability to require central banks to monitor and gather data about the microcredit sector. This requirement further legitimizes the work of microcredit banks.

Aside from the public accolades for microcredit, it is the human side that is most indicative of success. Created to empower the poor microcredit provides access to funds, extends trust, forges a stronger sense of community, and, perhaps most importantly, allows individuals to live with dignity.

Consider the experiences of Makeda (a composite of many women whose lives have been positively affected by microcredit), who lives in eastern Ethiopia. Her small village, located near the city of Domo, is home to many subsistence farmers. Like them, she supports herself and her children by growing maize (corn). With the advent of a local microcredit program, however, she obtains a loan, the equivalent to US$50, which enables her to rent a larger tract of land, harvest and sell more maize, and purchase livestock, including a goat and five chickens for milk and egg production. By American standards this loan may seem to be a modest figure; however, for Makeda, her family, and her community, replacing subsistence farming with surplus production represents autonomy and opportunity.

INTERNATIONAL ORGANIZATIONS AT WORK: INSPIRATION FOR CHANGE

The variations within and across Africa and Asia are vast; however, these continents offer locally and globally informed communities wherein the World Bank and the IMF programs are at work. The ongoing review of these initiatives, especially in light of the proposed realization of the UN's ambitious Millennium Development Goals, provides opportunities for program critiques and reforms to meet specific needs. Rather than seeing poverty reduction and development as "one size fits all" objectives, Africa and Asia, like other developing parts of the world, necessitate responsive policies, ones in which the human faces and realities of development are at the forefront of program planning and delivery.

5

The Future of the World Bank and the International Monetary Fund

GLOBALIZATION HAS MADE THE WORLD AN INTERCONNECTED place. As innovations and crises in one part spread rapidly, the entire world feels the implications. Poverty reduction and debt promotion are no different. Although a country like the United States may seem to be far removed from these issues, especially given its prominence as the world's largest and most influential economy, it is also drawn in. As the largest and one of the most influential members of the World Bank and the IMF, the United States must consider its role within these organizations, the future of these organizations, and the changing nature of globalization. Although new political administrations do inform how the United States negotiates its relationship with these global institutions, whether it retreats into greater

(continues on page 92)

GLOBAL FOOD SECURITY—
A CHALLENGE FOR THE FUTURE

Going to the local grocery store provides a lesson in world politics, cultural diversity, and economics. The availability of products
from local and international suppliers, what these food items tell
us about the cultures in which they are produced, and the costs of
these items are indicators of political, cultural, and economic systems. Prices for food staples or commodities, including corn, wheat,
rice, and coffee, have increased. During 2008, for example, wheat
has doubled in price in less than a year. Rice and coffee are trading

(continues)

At this Queens, New York, grocery store, customers are limited to purchasing two bags of rice due to the price increase of U.S. long-grain rice by 61 percent in 2008.

(continued)

at 10-year-high levels. A visit to the grocery store reveals the two primary consequences for consumers: increased prices and empty store shelves as some products become harder for stores to supply.

For Kevin, a high school student living in Seattle, food prices and availability are not priorities for him. Although more interested in the price of the latest video game than the price of rice, he is seeing the realities of global interconnections. Working part-time at the local food mart to make some money to support his love of the latest video games, he spends five afternoons a week stocking shelves, bagging items, helping customers carry their purchases to their cars, making deliveries, and operating the cash register. He notices that the rice shelf is almost empty. Being conscientious, he goes to the storage area at the back of the store to look for more rice. Strangely, he sees none. Asking his manager about the lack of rice, she informs him that the store has not received any rice shipments from the central distribution warehouse during the past week. Rice shipments, provided new suppliers can be found in Asia, should resume the following week.

Returning to the rice section, this time with a bright yellow sign in hand indicating that the store regrets the inconvenience of the missing product, Kevin sees something unusual. To his surprise, he sees two customers, apparently in a race to fill their shopping carts with the remaining bags of rice. Fortunately, this strange competition did not lead to violence since both shoppers were able to buy rice. Later that night, Kevin sees food riots on the television news. Images of armed soldiers protecting rice storage facilities, people pushing forward in food distribution lines, and anxious faces remind him of the strange competition he witnessed in the rice aisle earlier that day.

Bombarded with telephone calls, faxes, and e-mails, Sampaguita, a distribution specialist for one of the largest rice producers in the Philippines, is stressed. Named after the national flower of the Philippines, Sampaguita has felt a life-long connection to the land. Today, sadly, that connection is a source of anxiety for her. Fielding calls from a large number of current and prospective buyers, including a supermarket chain in Seattle and local community groups in Manila seeking a secure supply of rice, she is feeling the impacts of global food security on a personal level. Working cooperatively with the Philippine government, Sampaguita's company is to trying to ensure the safe and equitable distribution of rice throughout the country. The company hired additional security guards to work with military personnel to protect the rice storage facility. While the image of armed soldiers is disconcerting for Sampaguita, just as it was for Kevin in Seattle, their presence helps to prevent food riots. Some local residents have asked their relatives, many of whom live in the United State, to send care packages containing rice, flour, and other food staples.

Increasing prices and reduced supply are the result of several contributing factors. Increasing global population growth, projected to increase to 9 billion people by 2050, creates greater demand for food, along with more pressure on land, water, petroleum (for fertilizers and to operate farm equipment), and food reserves. Environmental challenges of climate change, global warming, and desertification also occur as the land is placed under greater stress to supply the food needs of a growing global population. The growth of crops for biofuel production creates additional challenges. For instance, corn is used to produce ethanol; however, biofuel production reduces the amount of land available to grow crops for

(continues)

(continued)

human consumption. The emergence of an affluent middle class in China and India, in particular, and higher levels of food consumption in developed countries means that these consumers seek to purchase more food products.*

The World Bank and the IMF are working with local food producers and governments to ensure increased supplies and access to these food staples; however, critics contend that the preference for cash crops, including corn and sugarcane for biofuels, a trend dictated by World Bank policies, is contributing to food insecurity. The IMF is also working to ensure greater price stability and financial incentives for local farmers to produce staple crops for human consumption. Especially in this era of sustainability for development (making environmental and planning decisions today that will have positive impacts now and into the future), innovative leadership by local communities, governments, the World Bank, and the IMF is needed to ensure that a wide range of solutions are developed to respond to the issue of food security.

---

* World Bank. "Rising Food Prices." Available online at *http://72.14.205.104/ search?q=cache:y622vOq1llsJ:siteresources.worldbank.org/NEWS/Resources/ risingfoodprices_backgroundnote_apr08.pdf+rising+world+food+prices+world+bank &hl=en&ct=clnk&cd=1&client=safari.*

(continued from page 88)
isolationism or expands its influence, global economic stability, growth, and safety are of interest to American lawmakers and individual citizens, no matter what their political affiliations may be. The World Bank and the IMF also grapple with these overarching concerns, but from a global perspective.

In spite of concerns about food security, just one contemporary global issue in the news, development and poverty reduction figures are promising. For instance, world output growth rate (the total sum of all economic and industrial activity) continues to be at its highest rate in over three decades, now at 5 percent.[54] At the same time, increasing population, food demands, and environmental challenges place new and ever-changing pressures upon the World Bank and the IMF. These institutions need to be globally responsive to these changing needs.

The World Bank and the IMF provide global frameworks for action. Resisting simple answers to the complex challenges of poverty and underdevelopment, these institutions provide sites for local-national-global connectivity to identify and respond to problems. Within these institutions, activism, critical reflection, program development and implementation, community involvement, and capacity building assume prominence. Through an increasing global awareness and a critically informed dialogue, the World Bank and the IMF allow us to envision and, hopefully, realize a world wherein all of us, whether in developing or developed countries, are moving from poverty to development, from deprivation to plenty, and from silence to political and social activism for positive change.

1929–1939	Great Depression.
1939	World War II begins.
	Forty-four member nations sign the first Articles of the Agreement of the International Monetary Fund (IMF).
1944	International Bank for Reconstruction and Development (IBRD) is founded.
1945	The IMF's Articles of Agreement go into effect.
	World War II ends.
1946	Board of Governors holds its first meeting in Savannah, Georgia.
	Twelve executive directors of the IMF hold their first meeting in Washington, D.C.
1947	The IMF begins its operations.
	IBRD begins operations with 36 member countries.
	France becomes the first client of both the World Bank and the IMF, receiving a loan for $250 million.
1948	World Bank provides its first development loan of $13.5 million to Chile.
1951	Finland and Yugoslavia are the first countries to repay their loans to the World Bank in full.
1963	World Bank begins funding of accessible education.
1973	The Organization of the Petroleum Exporting Countries (OPEC) enacts oil embargo, raising oil prices and reducing oil supply.
1974	OPEC ends the oil embargo.
	IMF creates the Oil Facility, a fund to assist countries facing large oil bills as a result of the oil embargo.
1975	IMF expands the Oil Facility.

1985   U.S. President Ronald Reagan and the last general secretary of the Communist Party of the Soviet Union, Mikhail Gorbachev, meet to discuss arms reductions and renewal of cultural ties.

1991   Gorbachev dissolves the Soviet Union.

1996   Heavily Indebted Poor Countries Initiative (HIPC) is established.

1997   African Virtual University (AVU) is founded by the World Bank in Washington, D.C.

1998   World Bank establishes the Development Marketplace Awards.

Poverty Reduction Strategy Paper is introduced.

2000   United Nations Millennium Declaration outlines a series of goals with which to end poverty, later known as the Millennium Development Goals (MDGs).

World Bank launches the Africa Multi-Country HIV/AIDS Program (MAP); Meltzer Report offers criticism of Structural Adjustment Programs by the World Bank and the IMF.

2002   World Bank establishes the Children and Youth Unit.

2003   World Bank holds the first Youth, Development, and Peace Conference in Paris, France.

2004   Global Monitoring Report is introduced to check on MDG progress.

2005   G-8 countries agree to forgive the debts of the 18 most heavily indebted low-income countries.

2006   Dr. Muhammad Yunus wins the Nobel Peace Prize for his microcredit work.

2007   Robert B. Zoellick assumes the role of president of the World Bank; Dominique Strauss-Kahn assumes the role of managing director of the IMF.

2008   Petroleum hits $100 per barrel for the first time.

Stock markets around the world decline in response to fears about a U.S. recession after the sub-prime mortgage financial crisis.

Union of South American Nations is created—a joining together of the Andean Community and Mercosur economic blocs.

NOTES

Introduction

1. "Preliminary Assessment of the Macroeconomic Impact of the Tsunami Disaster on Affected Countries, and of Associated Financing Needs," International Monetary Fund. Available online at http://www.imf.org/external/np/oth/2005/020405.htm.

2. "Data and Statistics." The World Bank. Available online at *http://web.worldbank.org/WBSITE/EXTERNAL/DATA STATISTICS/0,,contentMDK:20420458~menuPK:641331 56~pagePK:64133150~piPK:64133175~theSitePK:239419, 00.html.*

3. Gregory Mock. "How Much Do We Consume?" Earth Trends—World Resources 2000–2001. Available online at *http://64.233.169.104/search?q=cache:FGbkWmOXezQJ: earthtrends.wri.org/pdf_library/feature/ene_fea_consume. pdf+world+bank+twice+as+much+fish+twice+as+much+ grain&hl=en&ct=clnk&cd=2&gl=ca.*

4. "Analyzing Poverty," World Bank. Available online at *http://web.worldbank.org/WBSITE/EXTERNAL/TOPICS/ EXTPOVERTY/EXTPA/0,,contentMDK:20202211~menu PK:435069~pagePK:148956~piPK:216618~theSitePK:430 367,00.html.*

5. "Education For All (EFA)," World Bank. Available online at *http://web.worldbank.org/WBSITE/EXTERNAL/ TOPICS/EXTEDUCATION/0,,contentMDK:20374062~ menuPK:540090~pagePK:148956~piPK:216618~theSite PK:282386,00.html.*

6. Nabil Sukkar, "The Digital Divide and Development," Mediterranean Development Forum, October 6–9, 2002. Available online at *http://64.233.169.104/search?q=cache: _8oGxWYg1tQJ:worldbank.org/mdf/mdf4/papers/sukkar. pdf+digital+divide+world+bank&hl=en&ct=clnk&cd= 2&gl=ca.*

7.   "Getting to Know the World Bank: A Guide for Young People," World Bank. Available online at *http://64.233.169.104/search?q=cache:EewOSBzKdWQJ:youthink.worldbank.org/4teachers/downloads/getting-to-know.pdf+6+million+youth+disabled+and+12+million+homeless+as+a+result+of+war+world+bank&hl=en&ct=clnk&cd=2&gl=ca.*

8.   Ibid.

9.   "What's the Issue?" World Bank—Youthink! Available online at *http://youthink.worldbank.org/issues/index.php.*

10.   Kofi Annan. "We the Peoples: The Role of the United Nations in the Twenty-first Century." Millennium Report of the Secretary-General of the United Nations. Available online at *http://un.org/millennium/sg/report/ch2.htm.*

11.   Ibid.

Chapter 1

12.   "About Us," World Bank. Available online at *http://web.worldbank.org/WBSITE/EXTERNAL/EXTABOUTUS/0,,pagePK:50004410~piPK:36602~theSitePK:29708,00.html.*

13.   "East Asia and Pacific Update—Testing Times Ahead," April 2008. World Bank. Available online at *http://web.worldbank.org/WBSITE/EXTERNAL/COUNTRIES/EASTASIAPACIFICEXT/TEAPHALFYEARLYUPDATE/0,,menuPK:550232~pagePK:64168427~piPK:64168435~theSitePK:550226,00.html*

14.   Amartya Sen, *Development as Freedom.* New York: Anchor Books, 2000, pp. 2–4.

15.   "A Dollar a Day: Finding Solutions to Poverty." World Bank and IMF. Available online at *http://library.thinkquest.org/05aug/00282/gov_worldbank.htm.*

16.   "Lending Rises, Quality Remains High-World Bank Releases Results for FY05," World Bank. Available online at *http://web.worldbank.org/WBSITE/EXTERNAL/NEWS/0,,contentMDK:20582147~pagePK:64257043~piPK:437376~theSitePK:4607,00.html.*

17. "The IMF and Serbia," International Monetary Fund—National Bank of Serbia. Available online at *http://64.233.169.104/search?q=cache:bZwSN5V7G00J: www.imf.org/external/country/SCG/rr/2006/121806. pdf+imf+quotas+totalling+%24317+billion&hl=en&ct=cl nk&cd=1&gl=ca.*

18. "650 Million Children Live on Less than $1 a Day," United Nations Childrens Fund-Information Newsline. Available online at *http://www.unicef.org/newsline/pr11.htm.*

19. "The IMF and Serbia," IMF.

20. Martin Gurria and Alec Ian Gershberg, "Costing the Education MDGs: A Review of the Leading Methodologies." World Bank on behalf of the Fast Track Initiative Partnership. Available online at *http://64.233.169.104/ search?q=cache:FSFYzl9LPz0J:www1.worldbank.org/edu- cation/efafti/documents/CostingeducationMDG.pdf+acces s+to+education+mdg+will+cost+%249.1+to+%2438+billi on&hl=en&ct=clnk&cd=1&gl=ca.*

21. "Working for a World Free of Poverty," World Bank Group. Available online at *http://64.233.169.104/ search?q=cache:X81lKN2JCRQJ:siteresources.worldbank. org/EXTABOUTUS/Resources/WorldBank.ppt+%2440+b illion+world+bank+since+1963&hl=en&ct=clnk&cd=1& gl=ca.*

22 "Health, Education, and Gender," World Bank Annual Report 2007. Available online at *http://web.worldbank. org/WBSITE/EXTERNAL/EXTABOUTUS/EXTANNREP/ EXTANNREP2K7E/0,,contentMDK:21491357~menuPK: 4232732~pagePK:64168445~piPK:64168309~theSitePK: 4077916,00.html.*

23. "Putting 550,000 More Children in Primary School in Burkina Faso," International Bank for Reconstruction and Development/World Bank. Available online at *http:// siteresources.worldbank.org/EXTANNREP2K7/Resources/ AR07-AWP-005-002-PP3.htm.*

Chapter 2

24. Robert Jonas is not an actual person. He is a composite of experiences from the Great Depression.

25. "History of the GI Bill," U.S. Department of Veterans Affairs. Available online at *http://www.gibill.va.gov/*.

26. "The Baby Boom: 1946 to 1964," *The First Measured Century*. PBS. Available online at *http://www.pbs.org/fmc/ timeline/dbabyboom.htm*.

27. D. H. Aldcroft. *The British Economy, Vol. 1. The Years of Turmoil, 1920–1951*. London: Wheatsheaf, 1986, pp. 15–27.

28. "Articles of Agreement," World Bank Group. Available online at *http://web.worldbank.org/WBSITE/EXTERNAL/ EXTABOUTUS/0,,contentMDK:20040600~menuPK:34625 ~pagePK:34542~piPK:36600~theSitePK:29708,00.html*.

29. "World Bank Group Historical Chronology, 1944–1949," World Bank. Available online at *http://web.worldbank.org/ WBSITE/EXTERNAL/EXTABOUTUS/EXTARCHIVES/0,, contentMDK:20035657~menuPK:56307~pagePK:36726~ piPK:437378~theSitePK:29506,00.html*.

30. "Articles of Agreement of the International Monetary Fund," International Monetary Fund. Available online at *http://www.imf.org/external/pubs/ft/aa/index.htm*.

31. "Senegal: Statistical Appendix," International Monetary Fund. Available online at *http://www.imf.org/external/ pubs/cat/longres.cfm?sk=16632.0*.

32. "Debt Relief Under the Heavily Indebted Poor Countries (HIPC) Initiative," International Monetary Fund. Available online at *http://www.imf.org/external/np/exr/facts/ hipc.htm*.

Chapter 3

33. "About Us," World Bank.

34. George Dei, *Schooling and Education in Africa: The Case of Ghana*. Trenton, N.J.: Africa World Press, 2004, p. 27.

35. "IMF Emergency Assistance: Supporting Recovery from Natural Disasters and Armed Conflicts," IMF. Available online at *http://www.imf.org/external/np/exr/facts/conflict.htm.*

36. "The Poverty Reduction and Growth Facility (PRGF)," IMF. Available online at *http://www.imf.org/external/np/exr/facts/prgf.htm.*

37. "Heavily Indebted Poor Countries (HIPC) Debt Initiative: Completion Point Documents," IMF. Available online at *http://www.imf.org/external/np/hipc/index.asp?view=com&sort=cty.*

Chapter 4

38. "Bank Hones Plan to Accelerate Progress in Africa," World Bank—The Africa Action Plan. Available online at *http://web.worldbank.org/WBSITE/EXTERNAL/COUNTRIES/AFRICAEXT/0,,contentMDK:20687937~menuPK:258649~pagePK:146736~piPK:226340~theSitePK:258644,00.html.*

39. Ibid.

40. "Doha Development Agenda: Negotiations, Implementation, and Development," World Trade Organization. Available online at *http://www.wto.org/english/tratop_e/dda_e/dda_e.htm.*

41. Ibid.

42. "IMF Concludes Article IV Consultation with Burkina Faso," IMF. Available online at *http://internationalmonetaryfund.com/external/np/sec/pn/2000/pn0057.htm.*

43. "Facts and Figures: The Cotton Trade," *Now*, PBS. Available online at *http://www.pbs.org/now/shows/310/cotton-trade.html.*

44. Vandana Shiva, "Towards a People Centered Fair Trade Agreement on Agriculture," Countercurrents.org. Available online at *http://www.countercurrents.org/en-shiva130104.htm.*

45. Ibid.

46. Jean-Baptiste M. P. Compaoré. Letter of Intent from the Government of Burkina Faso to the IMF, October 18, 2002. Available online at *http://imf.org/external/np/loi/2002/bfa/02/index.htm*.

47. Jan Pronk, "Globalization as Global Exclusion," *Globalization with a Human Face—Benefitting All*, UNU/UNESCO International Conference. Available online at *http://un esdoc.unesco.org/images/0013/001355/135505e.pdf*.

48. Economic Commission for Latin America and the Caribbean (ECLAC). *Globalization and Development*, Buenos Aires: ECLAC, 2002.

49. "Sub-Saharan Africa: A 2008 Report on the Global AIDS Epidemic," UNAIDS. Available online at *http://www.unaids.org/en/CountryResponses/Regions/SubSaharan Africa.asp*.

50. "In September 2000, the Bank launched the Multi-Country HIV/AIDS Program for Africa (MAP)," World Bank. Available online at *http://web.worldbank.org/WBSITE/EX-TERNAL/COUNTRIES/AFRICAEXT/EXTAFRHEANUT-POP/EXTAFRREGTOPHIVAIDS/0,,contentMDK:2041573 5~menuPK:1001234~pagePK:34004173~piPK:34003707~th eSitePK:717148,00.html*.

51. "Sub-Saharan Africa: A 2008 Report on the Global AIDS Epidemic," UNAIDS.

52. "Grameen Bank," Banglapedia: National Encyclopedia of Bangladesh. Available online at *http://banglapedia.org/HT/G_0192.htm*.

53. "Does Micro-credit Empower Women: Evidence from Bangladesh, Volume 1," World Bank Development Research Group. Available online at *http://econ.worldbank.org/external/default/main?pagePK=64165259&theSitePK =469372&piPK=64165421&menuPK=64166093&entityI D=000094946_03040104075225*.

Chapter 5

54. "Global Output Totals $59 Trillion—Developing Countries
     Have Increasing Share, Says World Bank," World Bank.
     Available online at *http://web.worldbank.org/WBSITE/
     EXTERNAL/NEWS/0,,contentMDK:21726167~pagePK:
     64257043~piPK:437376~theSitePK:4607,00.html.*

BIBLIOGRAPHY

Aldcroft, D. H. *The British Economy, Volume I: The Years of Turmoil, 1920–1951*. London: Wheatsheaf, 1986, 15–27.

Alston, P., Tobin, J., and Darrow, M. *Laying the Foundation for Children's Rights*. Florence, Italy: UNICEF/Innocenti Project, 2005.

Aninat, E. "The Process of Globalization." In *Globalization with a Human Face: Benefiting All* (pp. 12–19). Paris: UNESCO, 2004.

Annan, K. A. *We the Peoples: The Role of the United Nations in the 21st Century*. New York: United Nations, 2000.

———. *In Larger Freedom: Toward Development, Security and Human Rights for All*. Report of the Secretary-General of the United Nations. New York: United Nations, 2005.

Birdsall, N., R. Levine, and A. Ibrahim. *Toward Universal Primary Education: Investments, Incentives, and Institutions*. London: Earthscan, 2005.

Compaoré, J. B. *Letter of Intent from the Government of Burkina Faso to the IMF*, 2004. Available online. URL: http://www.imf.org/external/np/loi/2002/bfa/02/index.htm.

Cornia, G. A., Jolly, R., and Stewart, F., eds. *Adjustment with a Human Face*, Volume 1. Oxford University Press, 1987.

———. *Adjustment with a Human Face: Country Case Studies*. Volume 2. Oxford: Oxford University Press, 1988.

Dei, G. *Schooling and Education in Africa: The Case of Ghana*. Trenton, N.J.: Africa World Press, 2004.

Economic Commission for Latin America and the Caribbean (ECLAC). *Globalization and Development*. Buenos Aires: ECLAC, 2002.

Friedman, T. *The World Is Flat: A Brief History of the Twenty-first Century*. Vancouver, BC: Douglas & McIntyre, 2007.

Grameen Bank. *Profit and Loss Account for the Year Ending 31 December 2006*. Dhaka, Bangladesh: Grameen Bank, 2007.

Grossholtz, J. "The Cotton Campaign." 2004. Available online. URL: http://www.wloe.de/pdf/voicesofwomen/jeangrossholtz.pdf.

Hogan, M. J. *The Marshall Plan: America, Britain, and the Reconstruction of Western Europe, 1947–1952*. Cambridge: Cambridge University Press, 1987.

International Labor Organization. *A Fair Globalization: Creating Opportunity for All*. Geneva: ILO, 2004.

International Monetary Fund. *Globalization: Threat or Opportunity, an IMF Issues Brief*. Washington, D.C. 2000. Available online. URL: http://www.imf.org/external/np/exr/ib/2000/041200to.htm\. For additional reading, see URL: http://www.imf.org/external/np/exr/key/global.htm.

———. *Annual Report*. 2006.

———. *Annual Report*. 2007.

———. *Annual Report*. 2008.

Isard, P. *Globalization and the International Financial System: What's Wrong and What Can Be Done*. Washington, D.C.: IMF, 2005.

Jayasuriya, R., and Wodon, Q. *Efficiency in Reaching the Millennium Development Goals*. Washington, D.C.: World Bank, 2003.

Jochnick, C. "Confronting the Impunity of Non-State Actors: New Fields for the Promotion of Human Rights." *Human Rights Quarterly*, 21(1), 1999, 56–79.

Jones, L. Y. "Swinging 60s?" *Smithsonian*, January 2006, 102–107.

Jones, P. W. *The United Nations and Education: Multilateralism, Development, and Globalization*. London: Routledge/Falmer, 2005.

Judt, T. *Postwar: A History of Europe Since 1945*. New York: Penguin, 2006.

Klein, N. *No Space, No Choice, No Jobs, No Logo: Taking Aim at the Brand Bullies*. Toronto: Vintage, 2000.

Lansdown, G. *The Evolving Capacities of the Child*. Florence: UNICEF/Innocenti Project, 2005.

Lingard, B. "It Is and It Isn't: Vernacular Globalization, Educational Policy, and Restructuring." In *Globalization and Education: Critical Perspectives*, edited by N. Burbules and C. Torres. New York: Routledge, 2005.

Meltzer, A. H. *What Future for the IMF and the World Bank?* Washington, D.C.: World Bank, 2003.

Mutua, M. *Human Rights: A Political and Cultural Critique*. Philadelphia: University of Pennsylvania Press, 2002.

Pronk, J. "Globalization as Global Exclusion," in *Globalization with a Human Face: Benefiting All*, pp. 131–136, Paris: UNESCO, 2004.

Rao, R., and Smith, I. *Partnerships for Girls' Education*. London: Oxfam, 2005.

Sachs, J. D. *The End of Poverty: How We Can Make It Happen in Our Lifetime*. London: Penguin, 2005.

———. "The Development Challenge." *Foreign Affairs*, March/April, 2005: 78–90.

Said, Edward W. *Orientalism*, New York: Vintage, 1979.

Sen, Amartya. *Development as Freedom*. New York: Anchor Books, 1999.

Sengupta, A. "On the Theory and Practice of the Right to Development." *Human Rights Quarterly*, 4(24), 2002: 837–889.

Stiglitz, J. *Globalization and Its Discontents*. New York: Norton, 2002.

Stone, D. and Wright, C., eds. *The World Bank and Governance: A Decade of Reform and Reaction*. New York: Routledge, 2006.

Suarez-Orozco, M. M., and Baolin Qin-Hilliard, D., eds. *Globalization: Culture and Education in the New Millennium*. Berkeley and Los Angeles: University of California Press, 2004.

Tomasevski, K. *Education Denied: Costs and Remedies*. London: Zed Books, 2003.

UNESCO. *Education for All: Global Monitoring Report*. Paris: UNESCO, 2007.

UNICEF. *Adjustment with a Human face*. New York: UNICEF, 1987.

———. *Summary of the World Summit for Children*. New York: UNICEF, 1990.

———. *Building a World Fit for Children: The UN General Assembly's Special Session on Children, 8–10 May 2002*. New York: UNICEF, 2002.

———. *Implementation Handbook for the Convention on the Rights of the Child*. Geneva: UNICEF, 2002.

———. *UNICEF's Priorities for Children, 2002–2005*. New York: UNICEF, 2002.

———. *Gender Achievements and Prospects in Education*. New York: UNICEF, 2005.

———. "Progress for Children: A World Fit for Children— Statistical Review." Available online. URL: http://www. unicef.org/publications/files/Progress_for_Children_No_ 6_revised.pdf.

———. *The State of the World's Children*. New York: UNICEF, 2007.

United Nations. *Universal Declaration of Human Rights (UDHR), 1948*. UN GA Resolution 217 A (III). Available online. URL: http://www.un.org/Overview/rights.html

———. *Millennium Declaration*, 2000. UN Resolution A/RES/ 55/2. Available online. URL: http://www.un.org/millennium/ declaration/ares552e.htm.

———. *Millennium Development Goals*, 2000. UN Resolution A/56/326. Available online. URL: http://www.un.org/ millenniumgoals/.

———. *Global Agenda for Dialogue Among Civilizations*. New York: United Nations, 2001.

———. *World Youth Report*. New York: United Nations, 2007.

———. *The Millennium Development Goals Report*. New York: United Nations Department of Economic and Social Affairs, 2007.

Van Ginkel, H. "Mapping Globalization." In *Globalization with a Human Face: Benefiting All*. Paris: UNESCO, 2004.

World Bank. *Global Economic Prospects and the Developing Countries*. Washington, D.C.: World Bank, 2000.

———. *Atlas of Millennium Development Goals: Building a Better World*. Washington, D.C.: World Bank, 2005.

———. *Getting to Know the World Bank: A Guide for Young People*. Washington, D.C.: World Bank, 2005.

———. *Paris Declaration on Aid Effectiveness: Ownership, Harmonization, Alignment, Results, and Mutual Accountability*. Washington, D.C.: World Bank, 2005.

———. *Annual Report*. 2006.

———. *Annual Report*. 2007.

———. *Annual Report*. 2008.

———. *Rising Food Prices: Policy and Options—A World Bank Report*. Washington, D.C.: World Bank, 2008.

———. *East Asia: Testing Times Ahead.* Washington, D.C.: World Bank, 2008.

World Trade Organization. *Doha Declaration.* 2001. Available online. URL: http://www.wto.org/english/tratop_e/dda_e/dda_e.htm#dohadeclaration.

Wright, Shelley. *International Human Rights, Decolonization and Globalization: Becoming Human.* London: Routledge, 2001.

 # FURTHER READING

BOOKS AND ARTICLES

Friedman, T. *The World Is Flat: A Brief History of the Twenty-first Century.* Vancouver, BC: Douglas & McIntyre, 2007.

International Monetary Fund (THE IMF). *Annual Report.* Washington, D.C.: IMF, 2008.

Sachs, J. D. *The End of Poverty: How We Can Make It Happen in Our Lifetime.* London: Penguin Books, 2005.

Sen, A. *Development as Freedom.* New York: Anchor Books, 1999.

Stiglitz, J. *Globalization and Its Discontents.* New York: Norton, 2002.

World Bank. *Getting to Know the World Bank: A Guide for Young People.* Washington, D.C.: World Bank, 2005.

WEB SITES

African Virtual University
http://www.avu.org

This site provides a comprehensive overview of the work, objectives, and course offerings of the African Virtual University.

Cyber School Bus
http://cyberschoolbus.un.org/

Created and maintained by the United Nations, this site provides detailed overviews of a wide range of global issues for young adult readers.

Drishtee
http://www.drishtee.com

This site profiles the work and activism of Drishtee, a non-governmental organization dedicated to providing Internet access to rural India. Drishtee was awarded a Development Marketplace award to support its work.

Education and the World Bank

http://web.worldbank.org/WBSITE/EXTERNAL/TOPICS/EXTEDUCATION/
0,,menuPK:282391~pagePK:149018~piPK:149093~theSitePK:2823
86,00.html

This site provides a detailed overview of the World Bank's involvement with the Education for All (EFA) Initiative. EFA was created to support the Millennium Development Goal of universal primary education for all children by 2015.

Grameen Bank

http://www.grameen-info.org/

This site profiles the history of microcredit, with particular emphasis on the work and vision of Dr. Muhammad Yunus and the Grameen Bank.

The International Monetary Fund

http://www.imf.org/external/index.htm

This site provides an extensive overview of the mandate and functions of the IMF.

Multi-Country HIV/AIDS Program (MAP)

http://web.worldbank.org/WBSITE/EXTERNAL/COUNTRIES/AFRICAEXT/
EXTAFRHEANUTPOP/EXTAFRREGTOPHIVAIDS/0,,contentMDK:2041161
3~menuPK:717155~pagePK:34004173~piPK:34003707~theSitePK:
717148,00.html

With particular focus on the Africa Multi-Country HIV and AIDS Program (MAP), this site highlights the World Bank's efforts to address the spread of HIV and AIDS throughout Africa.

United Nations Millennium Development Goals
http://www.un.org/millenniumgoals/

This United Nations site profiles the eight Millennium Development Goals (MDGs). Assessment reports outlining the extent to which each goal has—or has not—been reached are also provided.

The World Bank
http://www.worldbank.org

This site provides an extensive overview of the mandate and functions of the World Bank.

YouThink!
http://youthink.worldbank.org/

Written for a young adult audience, this World Bank site highlights a variety of key development issues, including sustainability, accessible education, and gender equality. Using interactive stories, video clips, and quizzes, readers are invited to think about how these issues relate to the work of the World Bank.

Dr. Muhammad Yunus
http://www.muhammadyunus.org/

This site profiles the life and work of Dr. Muhammad Yunus, the founder of microcredit.

PICTURE CREDITS

INDEX

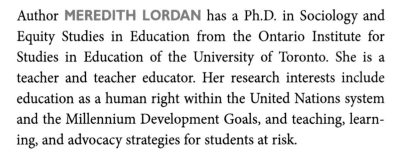

ABOUT THE CONTRIBUTORS

Author **MEREDITH LORDAN** has a Ph.D. in Sociology and Equity Studies in Education from the Ontario Institute for Studies in Education of the University of Toronto. She is a teacher and teacher educator. Her research interests include education as a human right within the United Nations system and the Millennium Development Goals, and teaching, learning, and advocacy strategies for students at risk.

Series editor **PEGGY KAHN** is a professor of political science at the University of Michigan–Flint, where she teaches world and European politics. She has been a social studies volunteer in the Ann Arbor, Michigan, public schools, and she helps prepare college students to become teachers. She has a Ph.D. in political science from the University of California, Berkeley, and a B.A. in history and government from Oberlin College.